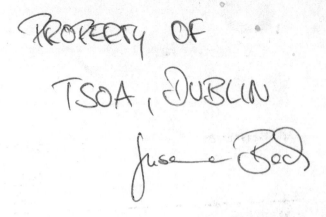
Contemporary Irish Filmmakers

Contemporary Irish Writers and Filmmakers

General Series Editor:
Eugene O'Brien, Head of English Department,
Mary Immaculate College, University of Limerick.

Titles in the series:

Seamus Heaney: Creating Irelands of the Mind
by Eugene O'Brien (Mary Immaculate College, Limerick)

Brian Friel: Decoding the Language of the Tribe
by Tony Corbett

Jim Sheridan: Framing the Nation by Ruth Barton
(University College Dublin)

John Banville: Exploring Fictions by Derek Hand
(Dun Laoghaire Institute of Art, Design and Technology)

William Trevor: Re-imagining Ireland by Mary Fitzgerald-Hoyt
(Siena College, New York)

Conor McPherson: Imagining Mischief by Gerald Wood
(Carson-Newman College, Tennessee)

Forthcoming:

Roddy Doyle by Dermot McCarthy

Neil Jordan by Emer Rockett and Kevin Rockett

Jennifer Johnston by Shawn O'Hare

Brian Moore by Philip O'Neill

Maeve Binchy by Kathy Cremin

John McGahern by Eamonn Maher

Colm Toibin by Declan Kiely

Contemporary Irish Filmmakers

Jim Sheridan

Framing the Nation

Ruth Barton

The Liffey Press

Published by The Liffey Press
307 Clontarf Road,
Dublin 3, Ireland
www.theliffeypress.com

© 2002 Ruth Barton

A catalogue record of this book is
available from the British Library.

ISBN 1-904148-05-0

Front cover photograph © Amelia Stein
Reproduced with the kind permission of the Irish Film
Archive of the Film Institute of Ireland

Printed in the Republic of Ireland by Colorman Ltd.

Contents

About the Author

Ruth Barton is IRCHSS (Irish Research Council for the Humanities and Social Sciences) post-doctoral research fellow at the Centre for Film Studies, University College Dublin. Her research interests include British and Irish cinema and she is currently working on a book entitled *Irish National Cinema* to be published by Routledge.

Series Introduction

Given the amount of study that the topic of Irish writing, and increasingly Irish film, has generated, perhaps the first task of a series entitled *Contemporary Irish Writers and Film-makers* is to justify its existence in a time of diminishing rain-forests. As Declan Kiberd's *Irish Classics* has shown, Ireland has produced a great variety of writers who have influenced indigenous, and indeed, world culture, and there are innumerable books devoted to the study of the works of Yeats, Joyce and Beckett. These writers spoke out of a particular Irish culture, and also transcended that culture to speak to the Anglophone world, and beyond.

Ireland, however, has undergone a paradigm shift in the last twenty years. Economically, politically and culturally, it is a vastly different place to the Ireland of Yeats and Joyce. In the light of the fundamentally altered nature of the Diasporic experience, definitions of Irishness and of identity are being rewritten in a more positive light. Irish people now emigrate to well-paid jobs, working in high rise offices in London and New York, a far cry from previous generations whose hard physical labour built those self-same offices. At the same time, the new-found wealth at home has been comple-mented by a growing multiculturalism, challenging perspec-tives on identity like never before.

Modes and worldviews inherited from the past no longer seem adequate to describe an increasingly cosmopolitan and complex society. This is the void which Contemporary Irish Writers and Filmmakers hopes to fill by providing an examination of the state of contemporary cultural Ireland through an analysis of its writers and filmmakers.

The role of the aesthetic in the shaping of attitudes and opinions cannot be understated and these books will attempt to understand the transformative potential of the work of the artist in the context of the ongoing redefinition of society and culture. The current proliferation of writers and filmmakers of the highest quality can be taken as an index of the growing confidence of this society, and in the desire to enunciate that confidence. However, as Luke Gibbons has put it: "a people has not found its voice until it has expressed itself, not only in a body of creative works, but also in a body of critical works," and Contemporary Irish Writers and Filmmakers is part of such an attempt to find that voice.

Aimed at the student and general reader alike, this series will analyse and examine the major texts, themes and topics that have been addressed by these present-day voices. At another level, each book will trace the effect of a specific artist on the mindset of Irish people.

It is hoped that this series will encourage discussion and debate about issues that have engaged the writers and filmmakers who enunciate, and transform, contemporary Irish culture. It is further hoped that the series will play its part in enabling our continuing participation in the great humanistic project of understanding ourselves and others.

Eugene O'Brien
Department of English
Mary Immaculate College
University of Limerick

Acknowledgements

I would like to thank Jim Sheridan for his co-operation with this book. I am especially grateful to Niamh Nolan of Hell's Kitchen and Renate Adamidov of the *East of Harlem* production office for their help with specific details. My thanks, too, to my colleagues at the Centre for Film Studies, UCD, Leon Conway, Margaret Brindley, Tony Fitzmaurice, Gerardine Meaney, Harvey O'Brien and also Susanne Bach for help and support. I would like to acknowledge the assistance of Grainne Humphries at the Film Institute of Ireland and Tony Deegan at RTÉ radio in obtaining research materials; also the help of the staff of the libraries of the British Film Institute, the Film Institute of Ireland and University College Dublin. Eugene O'Brien and Brian Langan have contributed to this book in many ways and with much good will, and I am indebted to them for that. Most particularly, thank you to Willie, Conal, Eoin and Paddy for putting up with it all.

This book was written under the Irish Research Council for the Humanities and Social Sciences post-doctoral research fellowship scheme.

Material from *The Gay Byrne Show* is reproduced with kind permission of RTÉ and Jim Sheridan.

For Willie, Conal, Eoin and Paddy

Chronology

1949	Jim Sheridan born in Dublin on 6 February. The eldest of seven children, his family lives in Seville Place, a working-class area on Dublin's Northside.
1957	Fianna Fáil is elected in the general election and remains in power until 1973.
1958	Publication of T.K. Whitaker's *Economic Development*, now widely associated with the beginning of the modernisation and industrialisation of Irish society.
1959	Seam Lemass becomes Taoiseach (prime minister) with Eamon de Valera elected President.
1961	RTÉ television begins broadcasting on New Year's Eve.
1967	Death of Frankie, Sheridan's younger brother, at the age of eleven; Northern Ireland Civil Rights Association is founded.
1972	Sheridan graduates from UCD; marries Fran; their first child, Naomi, is born; on 30 January, thirteen people taking part in a civil rights march are killed in Derry by the British Army in what becomes known as Bloody Sunday.
1973–74	Tours Ireland with Neil Jordan and their "Children's T Company."

1973	Wins the Macauley Fellowship in playwriting, the first time it has been awarded since Brian Friel won it in 1962.
1974	Bombs explode in Dublin and Monaghan, the eventual death toll is 33; on 5 October, two PIRA bombs explode without warning in Guildford killing five people and injuring 54; on 21 November, 19 people are killed and 182 injured in two pub bombs in Birmingham also planted by the PIRA; the "Guildford Four", "Maguire Seven" and "Birmingham Six" are arrested and eventually tried and convicted for bombing and conspiring with the "bombers".
1976	Birth of Sheridan's daughter, Kirsten, now a filmmaker.
1977	The "Dirty Protest" starts in Long Kesh (the Maze) prison.
1978	Sheridan plays the young Brendan Behan in *Borstal Boy*, produced by Noel Pearson.
1981	Sheridan leaves Ireland to manage the Irish Rebel Arts Center in New York City; changes the name to the Irish Arts Center. Republican prisoners begin a hunger strike, demanding political status; one of the strikers, Bobby Sands, is elected MP for Fermanagh-South Tyrone while on strike; he dies on 5 May. Nine more prisoners die before the hunger strike is called off in October.
1985	Sheridan's third daughter, Tess, is born; he publishes *Leave the Fighting to McGuigan* (biography of the boxer, Barry McGuigan). The Anglo-Irish Agreement is signed by Margaret Thatcher and Garret FitzGerald; sightings of moving statues in Republic of Ireland; Kerry Babies tribunal.
1989	*My Left Foot* is released in Ireland; the Guildford Four convictions are quashed.

1990	*My Left Foot* plays at the New York Film Festival to massive critical praise; it wins the New York Film Critics' award for "Best Film", is nominated for the Golden Globe awards and garners five Academy Awards nominations, winning Best Actor and Best Supporting Actress; *The Field* is released; Gerry Conlon's *Proved Innocent* is published; Mary Robinson is elected President of Ireland.
1991	*The Field* receives one Academy Award nomination (for Best Actor); the Birmingham Six are released and the Maguire Seven cleared by the Court of Appeal.
1992	*Into the West* is released.
1993	Sheridan and Arthur Lappin set up their production company, Hell's Kitchen; *In the Name of the Father* is released; the Irish Film Board is re-established and the tax-breaks scheme (Section 35) amended to encourage greater investment in indigenous Irish filmmaking.
1994	*In the Name of the Father* receives seven Academy Award nominations. Sheridan plays Jonathan Swift in Mary McGuckian's film, *Words Upon the Window Pane*; the ban on Sinn Féin broadcasts is let lapse in the Republic of Ireland; on 31 August, the PIRA announces a ceasefire; this is followed by a loyalist paramilitary ceasefire from midnight, 13 October.
1996	Sheridan appears in cameo roles in two films, *Moll Flanders* and *This is the Sea*.
1997	*Some Mother's Son* is released.
1998	*The Boxer* is the opening film at the Berlin Film Festival; and then opens on general release; the Belfast (Good Friday) Agreement is signed on 10 April; in August 28 people are killed and 360 injured when a bomb explodes in Omagh; the "Real IRA" claims responsibility.

1998 onwards	The Peace Process negotiations are carried out at a painfully slow pace with the issue of PIRA decommissioning remaining a major sticking point.
2000	*On the Edge* is released.
1999	Sheridan takes a cameo role in the film *When the Sky Falls*; *The Boxer* wins "Best European Film" at the Spanish Goyas; *Agnes Browne* is released.
2001–02	*East of Harlem* in production.

Introduction

I remember the excitement when *My Left Foot* won its two Academy Awards (Oscars). The difference in time between Dublin and Los Angeles meant that those who had sat up all night were first with the news; the rest of Ireland woke up to it on the morning of Tuesday, 27 March 1990. The early morning radio shows, television, and then the newspapers couldn't get enough of it. Brenda Fricker's acceptance speech, "Anyone who gives birth 22 times deserves one of these," and Daniel Day-Lewis's gleeful, "You've just provided me with the making of one hell of a weekend in Dublin," were repeated and repeated. On the flagship morning radio programme, *The Gay Byrne Show*, everyone agreed that it was a great day for the Irish. Much of the credit for the film's success was laid at the feet of producer Noel Pearson who, it was felt, had stuck it out in show business and now could deservedly enjoy his day in the sun. The happy recipients came on the line from the celebrations in Los Angeles, as did Bono and Bob Geldof; the Taoiseach (Prime Minister), Charles Haughey, appeared on air to congratulate them on producing a winner (and to dodge questions about the re-establishment of the Film Board, disbanded by him in 1987). His son, the Lord Mayor, popped up afterwards to offer his sincere congratulations and a listener sent in a ballad on the theme of the British appropriation of *My Left Foot*. "We're being offered all sorts of scripts," Jim Sheridan said, in response to Gay Byrne's questions, "but we want to do our own thing. We have our own stories to tell and we'll stick with that. I don't think we'll get too caught up in doing the Hollywood-style films. We'll do it on our own terms if we can." All were of one mind: that *My Left Foot* would put Ireland on the filmmaking map.

Like many of my generation of graduates, I had left Dublin in the early 1980s, not for lack of a job (although wisdom was suggesting to me that I was never going to hack it as a copywriter), but because the city seemed dull, restrictive and utterly provincial. Seven years later, I was back, in a rented house, with twin boys and their father. Luckily, we didn't have too much time to consider it, but if we had, we might have noticed that Dublin hadn't greatly changed in the interim. The twins, who were babies, didn't appreciate Jim Sheridan's big moment but, shortly, when they and their younger brother go to secondary school, they will be made to, since *My Left Foot* is now on the curriculum. It takes its place there alongside the works of Chinua Achebe, Jane Austen, Charles Dickens, Seamus Heaney, James Joyce, Arthur Miller, Gerard Manley Hopkins, John McGahern and Sophocles to name a few of the canonical authors and poets from whom Leaving Certificate students may make their choices when preparing for their final exam. Nor is it the only film on a course that also offers *On the Waterfront* (Elia Kazan, US, 1954), *Richard the Third* (Richard Loncraine, UK, 1995), *Strictly Ballroom* (Baz Luhrmann, Australia, 1992), *The Third Man* (Carol Reed, UK, 1949) and *Cinema Paradiso* (Guiseppe Tornatore, Italy/France, 1988).

The decision to integrate *My Left Foot* into the secondary curriculum is indicative of the sea change that has taken place in Irish cultural life in the years since it was released. Most third-level institutions here now offer film studies at one level or another, and those that don't are waking up to the fact that language and literature students are much more likely to be attracted to courses that offer film than those that rely on the old staples of Anglo-Irish literature and the great European modernist writers. That's not to rubbish these works; it is simply an acknowledgement of the dynamics of the contemporary university. Irish film studies, almost non-existent at the time of *My Left Foot*'s release, now boasts its own canon. A hierarchy of texts was established with the publication of Kevin Rockett, John Hill and Luke Gibbons' then definitive study of Irish cinema, *Cinema and Ireland* (1987), which simultaneously offered critiques of commercial British and American cinematic representations of Ireland, drew attention to the failure of successive Irish governments to establish an indigenous industry and lauded the small oeuvre of the country's first wave of independent filmmakers whose work tended towards the anti-establishment and the avant-garde. These films have remained crucial to the academic study of contemporary Irish film, as their centrality to Martin McLoone's recent survey of the subject, *Irish Film: The Emergence of a Contemporary Cinema* (2000) attests.

Apart from those first experimental filmmakers, the name that has most consistently attracted academic attention has been that of Neil Jordan, soon to be the subject of another publication in this series (Rockett and Rockett, 2002). Jordan's importance, both as an *auteur*, with a specific range of personal concerns that recur throughout his films, and as one of the key filmmakers of the contemporary period, is reflected by the critical interest his films have aroused in local and international academic writing. *The Crying Game* has been widely analysed as much for its depiction of gender and race as for its intervention in representations of the Northern Irish troubles (Zizek, 1993; Lloyd, 1999).

The Butcher Boy (Neil Jordan, US, 1997) is awarded an entire chapter in Martin McLoone's publication (above).

What place does Jim Sheridan occupy in this academic league table? As this book will argue, his contribution to the formation of and self-confidence in an Irish film industry has been remarkable. His films have won innumerable awards, including two Oscars. He has demonstrated that Irish stories can win world audiences and that Irish films can be profitable. Yet, his films have been discussed less as artistic works than as events — the film that kick-started the Irish film industry, the film that enraged the British establishment — and as vehicles for star performances, primarily those of Daniel Day-Lewis.

It is perhaps their very profitability that has rendered Sheridan's films suspect, even slightly tainted, in the eyes of the academic establishment. Here is someone who makes films to an unashamedly mainstream formula, and, as the interview that accompanies this book testifies, does so without apology. As Sheridan has discovered, if you want people to watch your work in large numbers, then you have to present it in a populist manner. Undue complications of theme and plot only distract the attention, hence his tendency to strip existing narratives of their peripheral characters and focus on one or two key protagonists. His films are text-based and actor-driven. They seldom obfuscate the issue and offer themselves to unambiguous readings that generally hinge upon a tale of triumph in the face of adversity.

This formulaic approach to material should, however, not blind film scholars to the importance of his work. Just as Hollywood cinema is studied for its universality, for its ability to articulate common anxieties, and analysed for its appeal, so Sheridan's films demand to be revisited for their unerring address to popular sentiment. Popular here is meant in both the social sense, "of the people", and in the less politically nuanced association of "liked by the general public".

The subtitle of this book — *Framing the Nation* — suggests that these works capture and articulate the national mood. This is a potentially dangerous assumption, given the right of the individual to distance themselves from any generic sense of national identity. Yet, Sheridan's films so effectively deploy archetypes common to Irish fictions — the strong mother, the emasculated son, and the disenfranchised father — that they demand an allegorical reading. Their commercial success, particularly with Irish audiences, suggests that they tell stories that people want to hear and see, and in a manner that engages the mass viewing public.

The secondary interpretation of the book's subtitle relates to Sheridan's often combative approach to British subject matter. He makes no secret, in interview, of his antipathy towards Britain and British audiences. One of his most controversial films remains *In the Name of the Father*, a production that enraged that most reliable of Establishment mouthpieces, the British conservative media. It is an unflinching indictment of that country's justice system (despite Sheridan's assertion in my interview with him that it made its representatives out to be more humane than they were), and a timely corrective to any lingering equating of Britishness with fair play.

This book's approach is to focus on Sheridan's filmic work; hence its division into chapters that coincide with film titles. I have taken a simple chronological trajectory through his work, with the first four chapters being devoted to his first four films as director and subsequently producer. So we start with *My Left Foot*, work through *The Field*, *In the Name of the Father* and *Some Mother's Son* (produced and co-scripted by Sheridan), and *The Boxer*. The final chapter focuses on another film that may rightly be associated with these, *Into the West*, which he scripted but did not direct.

Each chapter further uses the opportunity to focus on one film to suggest how that work may be read against the

social and cultural background in which it was made. Thus,
My Left Foot will be seen to reflect a tension between tradition and modernity that informed Irish society as it emerged
from a period in which the modernising process seemed to
have gone singularly awry. *The Field* will be read as a response to the crisis in historical representation engendered
by revisionism and a disavowal of the past, whilst *In the
Name of the Father* and *Some Mother's Son* will be analysed
for their intervention in the politics of the Troubles. *The
Boxer* is Sheridan's most recognisable genre film to date and
will be considered both in this light and as a "corrective" to
In The Name of the Father. Finally, *Into the West* will be seen
to deploy many of the signatures that were to become
trademarks of Sheridan's cinema, in particular his elevation
of the family to symbol of the nation. The book ends with an
interview with Sheridan in which he discusses his work, his
influences and his place within the wider Irish film industry.

Any reader wishing to learn about the more personal
details of the director's life will, therefore, have to look
elsewhere. The place to start is certainly with Peter Sheridan's memoir of his and his siblings' childhood, *44* (Sheridan,
1999), and its companion-piece, *Forty-Seven Roses* (2001). In
these narratives of growing up in Seville Place, near the
Sherrif Street flats, a working-class area of Dublin's north-
side, "Shea" makes brief appearances as a distant but ad-
mired older brother. Jim Sheridan was the eldest of the
seven children; their father worked as a clerk with the rail-
ways and, three nights a week, at the greyhound track; his
mother took in lodgers to pay for the children's education.
These combined incomes made them, according to Sheridan,
"the aristocrats" of their area (see interview). In his
brother's recollection, the eldest son occupied a privileged
position within the family:

> Ma told him everything. He was Ma's favourite and
> she never did anything to hide it. Shea always took
> Ma's part when she fought with Da. He was her little
> protector. She told him things she didn't even tell
> Da. (Sheridan, 1999: 12)

Their father is depicted as an impulsive autocrat whose bull-
ish temperament was often a front for a genial personality.
Comparing his own father with the overbearing fathers of so
many of his films, Sheridan has remarked that,

> the weird thing is that this didn't equate with my
> own father, who was essentially gentle. We had our
> rows . . . but much less than normal. I kept thinking,
> there's another father in my head, who's not my real
> father, why am I doing this? So I was looking for a
> story about a good father, and I found Guiseppe
> Conlon, and I think Da was aware of that.
>
> On the opening night of *In the Name of the Father*,
> I told the audience that Da was the model for
> Guiseppe and he was happy with that. He came up
> and gave me a big hug and said he loved me, and I
> said I loved him. (Woodworth, 1994: 1)

The formative occurrence of the Sheridans' childhood was
the death of their brother, Frankie, at the age of 11, from a
brain tumour. This constitutes the major crisis in Peter
Sheridan's book and is frequently alluded to by Jim. As a way
of responding to their loss, the Sheridans' father formed an
amateur theatrical company in which the whole family was
encouraged to take part. Although both Peter and Jim eventually moved away from acting to direction — Peter in the
theatre and Jim in both theatre and cinema — they both cut
their teeth on the boards of the Oriel Hall with the Saint
Laurence O'Toole's Musical and Dramatic Society (SLOT):

> It was almost as if drama was a way of putting the
> family back together. In many ways, I think that's
> what the films I have done are about. There is a
> trauma, and afterwards the family comes back to-
> gether. (ibid.)

This intersection between life and art informs Sheridan's
films, often to the point of constituting a conflict between
the story and its telling. Thus, for instance, in *In the Name of
the Father* where this bifurcation is most evident, the narrative of the Guildford Four's wrongful imprisonment becomes
subordinated to the working through of the father–son relationship, the retrieval of the family unit.

Other aspects of the director's life re-emerge in his
films, most prominently, the story of the working-class boy
made good. Starting with *My Left Foot*, Daniel Day-Lewis has
functioned as Sheridan's alter-ego; whether as a severely
handicapped child, a petty thief imprisoned for a crime he
did not commit, or an IRA activist who has turned his back
on violence, the parts inhabited by Day-Lewis pit the sup-
portive framework of the family against the prejudices and
often-unspoken norms of the wider society into which he
was born. Drawing on his own innate abilities, this travelling
character discovers that he is both separate from, and part
of, his environment; he may leave it physically but it will always define who he is.

In reality, director and star could not share more diverse
upbringings. Daniel Day-Lewis is the grandson of Michael
Balcon and Jill Balcon, whose names are synonymous with
British cinema. His other grandfather was the poet laureate
Cecil Day-Lewis. He was educated in the "progressive" British private secondary school, Bedales, after running away
from Sevenoaks School, and shortly afterwards embarked on
an acting career that embraced both the stage and the
screen. His chameleon performances were exemplified in a

sequence of early screen roles that saw him appear as the irredeemable "toff", Cecil Vyse, in *A Room With A View* (James Ivory, UK, 1985) and subsequently as a gay wide-boy in the race-comedy, *My Beautiful Laundrette* (Stephen Frears, UK, 1985). Meanwhile his stage performances encompassed a much-discussed Hamlet in 1989, which he walked out from after hallucinating about his late father on stage. In interview, he is chalk to Sheridan's cheese; appearing reluctant to comment on his career or his much speculated-on romantic and private life. Where Sheridan comes across as an affable family man, and an inveterate raconteur, Day-Lewis has remained an elusive subject, his "real" character utterly effaced as he immerses himself in each consecutive role.

We may trace this insider/outsider dichotomy in the Sheridan/Day-Lewis collaborations not just to the director's and star's backgrounds but also to Sheridan's own encounter with emigration. The experience of the immigrant abroad is central to *In the Name of the Father* and forms one of the themes of *The Boxer*. Sheridan himself left Dublin and spent a year in England after graduating from University College Dublin (UCD). He left Ireland a second time in 1980 in the wake of the debacle that accompanied the appearance of the "Gay Sweatshop" at Dublin's Project Theatre, with which he had long been associated. As one of the directors of the Project, Sheridan had overseen a series of avant-garde performances that had garnered the centre a reputation at the cutting edge of fringe art. Neil Jordan, Gabriel Byrne and Liam Neeson had all also been involved with the Project in the 1970s, but it was the controversy aroused by the gay theatre group that finally saw the end of the art centre's municipal funding. Sheridan moved to New York with his wife and two children where, alongside the traditional manual labouring jobs of the newly arrived emigrant, he became involved with the Irish Arts Center (then called the Irish Rebel Arts Center). These experiences form one strand of

East of Harlem (in production at the time of writing), whose narrative fuses Sheridan's own life with that of his parents. In this latest film, an immigrant Irish family settle illegally in New York City after the death of their child, Frankie, in Ireland. The film follows their encounter with a panoply of other immigrants as it works through their own bereavement and the premature birth of their next baby.

It was in New York that he met ex-political prisoner turned playwright, Terry George, with whom he was to collaborate in the trilogy of Troubles films, *In the Name of the Father, Some Mother's Son* and *The Boxer*. In New York, Sheridan completed his only formal film training, an eight-week production course at New York University.

His experiences in theatre may have convinced Sheridan that the only way to make a living was to move into the film world, but they also confirmed his remarkable ability to coax exceptional performances from the actors with whom he worked. This has become one of the defining features of a Jim Sheridan film, most commented on in the case of Daniel Day-Lewis, but also evident in the range of supporting roles that have won critical acclaim for their actors and resulted in a plethora of awards and nominations.

As a theatre director, Sheridan met with considerable recognition and became associated with an iconoclastic left-wing mode of production that may be traced back to his early days in student theatre at UCD (*Oedipus Rex* as a rock musical with the audience hanging from three-storey scaffolding) and was cemented by his and his brother, Peter's, work at the Project. His first international success, however, came with his direction of *My Left Foot*, a film that might have remained a minor television hit if it had not been for a combination of a classic story of victory over the odds, some remarkable acting, a script that managed to remain just on the right side of mawkish and the energies of its makers, Sheridan and impresario/producer, Noel Pearson.

To this list we might add the film's American distributors, Miramax Films, run by the hawks of independent cinema, the Weinstein brothers.

Sheridan and Pearson stayed together to make one further film, *The Field*, before parting company. Sheridan formed his own production company, Hell's Kitchen, where he moved to the position of co-producer of his films with Arthur Lappin, formerly line-producer on *My Left Foot* and *The Field*. Hell's Kitchen has been responsible not only for producing Sheridan's works but has also made Anjelica Huston's *Agnes Browne* (Anjelica Huston, Ireland, 1999), Peter Sheridan's *Borstal Boy* (Peter Sheridan, UK/Ireland, 2000) and *Bloody Sunday* (as co-producer; Paul Greengrass, Ireland/UK, 2002). Sheridan has also appeared as Jonathan Swift in *Words upon the Window Pane* (Mary McGuckian, Germany/Luxembourg, UK, 1994) and in cameo roles in *Moll Flanders* (Pen Densham, US, 1996), *This is the Sea* (Mary McGuckian, Ireland/US, 1996) and *When the Sky Falls* (John MacKenzie, Ireland/US, 1999). His daughter, Kirsten, has followed in the family's footsteps and is now a feature film director in her own right.

With his more politicised films, starting with *In the Name of the Father,* Sheridan found himself in the midst of a media storm. This, as it is detailed in Chapter Three, was to have consequences not only for his artistic practices but also defined the parameters within which filmmakers in general found themselves able to work when wishing to depict aspects of the Northern Irish Troubles. At the heart of much of the criticism his films evoked lay an unresolved worry about the role of the artist within political debate. Reading through the responses to his films, there is a sense that it is in some way indecent for a filmmaker, particularly one wedded to a populist aesthetic, to meddle in matters more properly considered to lie within the domain of politicians and historians. Yet it could be argued of all Sheridan's films that he was not initiating any new ideological viewpoint but simply reflecting some of the discursive currents circulating in Irish society at that moment.

The approach this book takes, therefore, is that Jim Sheridan's films may most fruitfully be read as constituting a dialogue with contemporary Irish culture as well as reflecting their maker's personal view of the world. Film studies purists may well have already balked at the notion of organising a book around one director. The "author", as we well know, is dead and the *auteurist* approach to cinema apparently buried in the same grave. The Romantic concept of the artist as originator and centre of creative production has been replaced by the idea of the text as cultural product. Thus, a film does not simply mirror society but responds to it, often unconsciously reflecting and reformulating ideas and anxieties that circulate within the wider context of its making. Cinema, as a collaborative medium, is susceptible to multiple influences, those of producers, financiers, scriptwriters, actors and technicians, as well as that of the director. Popular cinema as practised by filmmakers such as Sheridan must also integrate into its mode of address some anticipation of its audiences' expectations. It must predict how an audience will "read" it, and speak in a language that will have the widest possible address; hence the knowing deployment of archetypes, stereotypes and generic conventions.

In this maze of signification, the director emerges as simply a part of the whole. To organise a book around a specific director's work, therefore, is a risky proposition. It could be read as an almost desperate attempt to impose order on chaos, to seek out patterns and allocate a meaning system to otherwise conflicting influences. On the other hand, within contemporary cinema, as much as within the classic auteurist cinemas of the European tradition, the director retains at least symbolic significance, refusing to lie still in the *auteurist* grave. The inevitability with which interviews with Sheridan accompany the release of his films reflects the promotional value that certain directors still represent. A Jim Sheridan film *is* an event, particularly in Ireland, where news of the film's production, generally accompanied by a publicity still of the director organising the actors or behind the camera, will have been drip-fed to the media at strategic intervals prior to its release. More than that, a Jim Sheridan film brings with it ontological significance. At one level, it promises some engagement with or reflection on Irish society, and at another, the anticipation of another extraordinary acting performance, usually by Daniel Day-Lewis. With his multiple Oscar nominations and triumphs, Sheridan has also come to signify the potential for international recognition of the Irish film industry. The interview circuit provides the film's director, and occasionally its stars, with an opportunity to pre-empt or adjust interpretations of the film's meaning. If this may be opaque or controversial, the interview is an occasion for attempting to gain control of the meaning-making process.

Again, the idea that any work of art has a fixed meaning that the educated and inspired interpreter will extract and disseminate to the less intellectually endowed recipient has also had to be abandoned by academia. Meaning is now understood to be flexible and transitory. Individuals, according to multiple factors (of birth, education, gender, nationality, race and mood), will view, and arrive at, conflicting understandings of works of art, including films. Interpretation of Sheridan's cinema in this book therefore reflects the ideas of this author; how others have received his films is more difficult to establish. The most reliable record in this case is the newspaper or other review. Whilst a film critic will respond to a production in a manner conditioned by the same personal factors as any other member of the audience, they will also be writing (or speaking) in a way that anticipates the consent of their constituency, the up-market British reader, the American metropolitan consumer, the local Irish viewer, and so on; hence the use of popular film criticism within this book on occasions where it is felt that it will throw light on conflicting interpretations of Sheridan's films.

In person and in his films, Jim Sheridan is a natural raconteur. As he says, "You just make things that make it easier for people to get up and go home after the cinema. You just make it to make life easier" (see interview). He has taken Irish stories and retold them to audiences not just at home but in countries throughout the world. His is, indisputably, entertainment cinema. Yet it has resonances, as it is hoped this book will illustrate, far beyond the processes of buying and selling cinema tickets. Within the universal narratives that form the core of Sheridan's works lie a range of references that will carry meanings only available to local audiences. Thus, for example, *The Boxer* alludes to the history of the "hardman" and an indigenous boxing tradition that is specific to Northern Ireland. To domestic viewers, such a narrative will carry associations that will almost certainly completely elude spectators from different countries and cultures. In his filmmaking practice, Sheridan not only has confirmed the validity of local narratives; he has confronted many of the issues circulating within the Irish body politic. The next five chapters will explore the cultural significance of these films within the context of Irish society, north and south of the border, in the twentieth and twenty-first centuries.

Chapter One

My Left Foot (1989):
The Collision with Modernity

The Ireland of 1989, into which Jim Sheridan's first feature film, *My Left Foot*, was released, was a country in the midst of rapid change. On the brink of the economic miracle that was to become known as the Celtic Tiger, it had apparently joined late-twentieth-century life with a speed that left little scope for adjustment. From being a peripheral nation best known for its quaint countryside and pre-industrial pace of life, it had hurtled through a process of modernisation that saw all the old beliefs and certainties shaken to the core.

In this environment, Sheridan is an emblematic figure. In an environment that has tended to pay lip service to the notion of a meritocracy, he has demonstrated that enterprise has its rewards and that artistic practices, including film, need not be the preserve of the middle-classes. More controversially, he has consistently proved that Irish cultural production can appeal to the local whilst circulating within a global environment of capitalist exchange, namely the Hollywood film industry. Much of the debate about the new Ireland, an Ireland that has been largely fuelled by multinational corporate investment, has hinged around a profound anxiety about the ability of a small culture to retain its identity within the universalising practices of global capital. The corollary to this debate is to question what kind of identity Ireland had prior to its full-scale engagement with globalism and to ask how much of the "old" Ireland was worth clinging on to anyway. A further and related discourse has expressed concern as to who the beneficiaries of modernisation have been; in other words, whether the rising tide has indeed "lifted all boats".

This ambivalence about modernity lies at the heart of *My Left Foot*'s narrative, an irony, perhaps, given that the film was entirely financed by overseas' capital, in this case, that of British television. The film is set in the pivotal year of 1959, which, as we shall see below, is regarded as the point at which the Irish economy officially abandoned its old principles of self-sufficiency in favour of participation in the international market. Due to its flashback structure, much of the film is, however, set in the preceding decades, enabling it to cast a critical eye on the Ireland of those years. In order to understand better the social and economic background that informs this film and *The Field*, it is therefore necessary to recapitulate briefly the events of the time in which both films are primarily set. We will also briefly consider the debates that accompanied Ireland's movement from tradition to modernity.

The period after the establishment of the Irish Free State in the Treaty of 1921, and following the Civil War years of 1922–23, is notable more for its continuity than its break with the past. Until the late 1950s, Ireland remained a predominately rural country. Under its long-serving leader Eamon de Valera, the dominant party of this period, Fianna Fáil, pinned its faith on a policy of self-sufficiency. Industrialisation was neglected in favour of the development of the rural economy. Education and health were entrusted to the religious orders and few aspects of Irish social and political life escaped the attentions of the hierarchy.

The alternative to staying in Ireland was to leave, and thousands did. The most debilitating effect on the country during these early post-independence years was the continuing outflow of its population, many of whom sought to release their artistic and entrepreneurial energies in more rewarding climates. Although emigration reached its highest levels during the successive famines of the nineteenth century, it continued to provide a solution to chronic unemployment during the first decades of independence. Between 1841 and 1961, the Irish population fell from 6.5 million to 2.8 million (Tansey, 1998: 11).

In retrospect, this period in the evolution of the state has come to be regarded with some equivocation. Most consistently, it has been represented in recent fictions as an era of material and psychological deprivation. Frank McCourt's *Angela's Ashes* (1997) is just one of a number of such recreations. There is, however, a second school of thought that views the post-independence period as one of prelapsarian innocence epitomised, in this instance, by the popular writings of Alice Taylor whose "recollections of rural simplicity have struck a resounding chord with an Irish reading public which possesses an endless appetite for reassurance about the verities of times past" (Foster, 2001: 164).

The year 1958 is generally seen to mark the moment that the Irish government finally abandoned its old policies and embraced modernisation. In this year, the Department of Finance, under its new secretary T.K. Whitaker, published a study entitled "Economic Development" that laid out a programme to encourage investment in potentially productive areas of the economy, if needs be through appeal to foreign capital.

By the late 1960s the effects of this turnaround, combined with a general growth in the world economy, had resulted in the Republic of Ireland witnessing its first economic boom. A rise in exports, the sudden availability of high-quality, low-cost consumer goods, increased employment and income prospects transformed the country.

Modernity, however, came at a price. To many commentators, it seemed that the embrace of consumerism was matched by a corresponding loss of personal and communal values. This mood was intensified when, in the late 1980s, at the time of the making of *My Left Foot*, severe corrective measures were taken by Charles Haughey's Fianna Fáil party to right an economy that had apparently run out of control. Kieran Allen has summed up the consequences of Haughey's return to government:

> Hospital wards were closed and more than 20,000 public servants were made redundant. Incontinent old people were even rationed for the amount of protective nappies they might use. Yet, while Haughey spoke of the need for restraint to tackle "critical fiscal problems", he himself led a life of such unparalleled luxury that he did not need to pay attention to how his own personal finances were organised. (Allen, 2000: 13)

The media became the site for much of the public debate around the consequences of embracing modernisation. This was particularly the case when a succession of moves to liberalise the country's anti-abortion and divorce laws took centre-stage in the mid-1980s. Television, inevitably, was blamed for influencing public taste and promoting materialism. Writing in 1989, historian J.J. Lee railed against the Irish tendency towards begrudgery; always there, he claimed, it was inflamed through exposure to American materialism disseminated by television:

With a wider range of goods now available to be flaunted, petty personal rivalries could flourish at every level over a variety of consumer goods, from clothes to cars, to other consumer durables, to foreign holidays. Begrudgery now had a wider range of grievances on which to fester. The number of small institutions grew, both in the public and the private sectors, reproducing the circumstances that fostered the spread of envy and jealousy among shrivelled personalities. The number and aggressiveness of vested interests, whether within the expanded state sector, or outside it, grew appreciably. Pressure groups became, if not more insidious, certainly more blatant, expressing their demands more stridently, more self-righteously, and more avariciously, as they launched demand after demand for "our" money from a growing but ineffectual state. (Lee, 1989: 648)

Jim Sheridan's first feature film, *My Left Foot*, is, like the era from which it emerged, torn between the competing claims of tradition and modernity. Adapted from Christy Brown's book of the same title, the film tells the story of Brown's early childhood as a sufferer from cerebral palsy to the publication of his book and his encounter with the nurse whom, as the end titles tell us, he will marry. The screenplay was co-authored by Jim Sheridan and Irish novelist and screenwriter, Shane Connaughton. In common with much of Sheridan's future work, it is both documentary and fiction. The film is not in fact based exclusively on the book, *My Left Foot* (first published 1954), but also draws on Brown's other autobiographical work, *Down All the Days* (first published 1970). The film is primarily a celebration of triumph over adversity, a well-honed cinematic trope and, as we shall see below, something of the "flavour of the moment" in Hollywood in the late 1980s. Its remarkable commercial performance elevated it far beyond the small Irish story it also was.

It propelled its director into the filmmaking mainstream, awarding him the clout to pitch for Hollywood capital to subsidise further Irish films. More significantly still, for the beleaguered local filmmaking community, it established the viability of Irish cinema as a commercial and cultural investment. The corollary to this success was a certain academic distrust of Sheridan's work, a sense that he had "sold out" and that his films were compromised by their participation in the economic order of the global entertainment industry.

In interview, Sheridan has spoken of his desire to ensure that *My Left Foot* would not be over-literary. In particular, he was anxious to avoid the formal looseness of much contemporary literature by investing the screenplay with a classic cinematic three-act structure (itself, ironically, borrowed from the conventions of the nineteenth-century realist novel):

> Screenplays are more like architecture than art in the way that they convey to the readers important information on which they have to act. It is very difficult for them to be self-reflective. They need a structure like a building that people can work in. They must be as clear as a knife. You know you are in trouble if the dialogue carries the narrative. (Sheridan, 1989: 11–12)

My Left Foot does indeed follow a conventional trajectory of conflict and resolution; it further aligns itself to a mainstream tradition of realist filmmaking by the creation of an illusory verisimilitude. The film opens in 1959 at a fund-raising gala where Christy Brown (Daniel Day-Lewis) has been invited to read from his recently published autobiography, *My Left Foot*. The nurse who has been assigned to care for him, Mary Carr (Ruth McCabe), prompts him to tell her about the book. In response, the camera zooms in on one of Christy's paintings, used here to illustrate his memoir, and the first of a series of lengthy flashbacks ensues. In these flashbacks, we revisit Christy's childhood and adolescence and witness his struggle to achieve external recognition of his identity. The increasingly flirtatious encounter between Christy and Mary structures the drama and enables the film to provide a commentary on its own narrative progression.

My Left Foot ends where it began, at the dinner, with an additional coda providing the information that Christy and Mary did indeed marry, thus allowing for a double resolution: of Christy's desire to lead a "normal" heterosexual life, and of his artistic ambitions. The impression of authenticity is reinforced by this commentary and by the knowledge that there is a pre-existing "true story". In fact, the film is only very loosely based on *My Left Foot*, the book. It combines a number of key figures who assist Christy, principally those of Dr Collis, his sister-in-law, Eirene Collis, a cerebral palsy specialist, and Dr Warnants. Dr Eileen Cole (Fiona Shaw) of the film is completely fictitious; in the book, Christy first falls in love with a local girl, Jenny, and it is his realisation that she pities rather than loves him that causes one of his cyclical moments of self-loathing. A key feature of the book is his gradual understanding that his disability is no more or less extraordinary than that of millions of others, an insight gained through a cathartic trip to Lourdes and his introduction to the young children at the cerebral palsy clinic (which he does attend; in the film, he refuses to).

The filmic representation of Christy as a singular individual engaged in an existential battle to achieve selfhood locates him to a much greater extent in a tradition of Hollywood heroes, disabled or otherwise. The device of establishing his personal identity through confirmation of his sexual persona again places this film squarely within the mainstream. Another notable departure from the original text is the portrayal of Christy's father who, in the written version of *My Left Foot,* is a benign, if absentee figure. The

character in the film bears closer resemblance to the father
in Brown's subsequent autobiographical exercise, the scato-
logical, Behanesque *Down All the Days*; here he becomes a
man with "pint-hopes and whiskey-expectations" (Brown,
1970: 42) who beats his wife and daughters and souses himself in drink and self-pity. Although a succession of subjective
shots in the film suggests to the viewer that this is Christy's
story, told from his point of view, a number of the events
take place in his absence.

My Left Foot is thus a reminiscence, a personal and selec-
tive act of memory that borrows from the memories of others and fabricates where there are voids. This departure from
the originating text was little remarked upon when the film
was released; on the contrary, many reviewers assured their
readers that this was a "true story". Assumptions of veracity
were reinforced by the film's realist aesthetic. Camera angles,
editing, set design, costume and, particularly, the acting of
Daniel Day-Lewis, all conspire to create an illusion of truth, a
statement that "this is how it happened". If such a strategy
was unremarkable in this instance, it was this insouciance over
historical accuracy that became one of the most controversial
aspects of Sheridan's entry into "political" filmmaking, as we
shall see in the case of *In the Name of the Father.*

The film's classical construction is matched by a functional shooting style. Sheridan and photographer, Jack Conroy, opt for a relatively static camera and a focus on people
rather than objects. In general, *My Left Foot* is dialogue-
heavy, with the camera holding the speakers in a two-shot
(with both simultaneously in view). Occasionally, this set-up
is abandoned for the subjective shot, as events are shown
from Christy's point-of-view; alternatively, a high-angled
viewpoint emphasises the young Christy's vulnerability as he
lies trapped on the floor.

Above all, this is an actorly film. Much was made in its
pre-publicity of Daniel Day-Lewis's involvement in the pro-

duction. Better known at that point as a Shakespearean actor, he spent eight weeks in a clinic to train for the part and
insisted on occupying his wheelchair throughout the shooting
day to adapt himself to Christy's conditions. He even painted
a number of the works seen in the film with his own left foot.
Sheridan's skill with, and foregrounding of, actors reflects his
theatrical background and this collaboration with Daniel Day-
Lewis was to be the first of several. Hugh O'Conor, as the
young Christy, turns in an equally strong performance, again
the subject of much praise from reviewers.

The opening sequences of *My Left Foot*, in which Christy
laboriously places a recording of *Cosi Fan Tutte* on the turn-
table and sits back to listen to it, establishes a mood of inti-
macy, focusing on Christy's individual struggle, which
characterises the remainder of the film. As a whole, the
work oscillates between a series of set-pieces that move the
action forward and lengthy intervals where the viewer is
locked into Christy's immediate environment. Possibly as a
consequence of its low budget or, equally, because of Sheridan's background in theatre, the film largely relies on the
interaction between individuals to establish its mood and
meaning. It is thus crucial that, from the beginning, it establish the identifying traits of its central characters and, in order to achieve this, Sheridan draws on a range of existing
archetypes with whom audiences might already feel some
sense of familiarity.

During the first flashback, we are introduced to Christy's
family, and their social background is sketched in. Dominat-
ing the household is the figure of Christy's mother. Physically massive — she is pregnant in the first scene and each
subsequent scene features a new baby — Mrs Brown
(Brenda Fricker) is the classic Irish matriarch of fiction and
ideology. She organises home, husband and children and is
alternatively patient and loving, critical and scolding. As
Catherine Nash has written:

In efforts to secure cultural autonomy and maintain
the cultural purity of Ireland after independence,
women became the measure of the nation. Their
idealisation as its mothers was evident in the anxieties expressed about foreign corruption of Irish
women. Foreign fashions, film, literature, music and
dance and foreign notions of sexual equality, it was
said, undermined the home and native honour towards women and degraded Irish women. (Nash,
1997: 115)

If Mrs Brown is drawn from the heart of the project of cultural nationalism that defined the period in which the early
parts of *My Left Foot* are set and to which Nash refers, she
also carries a symbolic weight that echoes through Irish historical representation. In effect, the character of Christy's
mother is severely over-determined. She is the classic "Irish
mammy", the tower of strength who must hold the family
together in the face of adversity — specifically, the Irish male
with his propensity to drink the meagre family income and
then engage in acts of domestic violence. Mrs Brown is associated exclusively with the domestic environment and her
own sexuality is seen solely as a conduit to childbearing. It is
no coincidence that her first name is Mary, and her role
within the film exemplifies the elision of the figures of Mary,
Mother of God with the traditional Irish mother, so common
in much literary, artistic and popular representation. It is Mrs
Brown who teaches Christy language, but at the point where
he can express himself (by writing on the blackboard) he is
able to join the company of men (the pub). She is also
Mother Ireland, the earth/mother to whom generations of
emigrant sons will always return for nurture, if not in body at
least in mind. C.L. Innes has identified in the symbolic figure
of Erin an ideal of Irish womanhood that was indebted to:

> hundreds of years of Irish history and cultural
> change, strands of which were focused upon and re-
> interpreted by both Anglo-Irish Protestant and
> Gaelic Catholic nationalists in the nineteenth and
> early twentieth centuries. Those strands include
> elements of ancient Irish mythology and legend, bal-
> lad and other oral folk traditions, including the
> Gaelic bardic traditions, the influence of the Catholic
> Church and the increasing stress in the nineteenth
> century on the worship of the Virgin Mary as Mother
> of God, the "Celtic Twilight" school popularized in
> England as well as Ireland by Thomas Moore, and the
> influence of English and European literary and artistic
> traditions with their uses of medieval and classical
> motifs and images. (Innes, 1993: 17–18)

All these influences come together in the fictional construction of Mrs Brown. This idealisation of the maternal figure
was to become an identifying feature of Sheridan's films, as
was his elision of mother with lover — *My Left Foot* closes
with the suggestion that, in another Mary (Carr), Christy will
have found a nurturing figure to replace his own mother.
The film's emotional core, and its most sentimental moments, are to be found in the tensions between his and his
mother's mutual love and in Christy's attempts to lay claim
to a form of masculinity that will enable him to replace his
father. In case this oedipal configuration should pass unno-
ticed, Sheridan himself underlines the message through a
sequence of interchanges between the characters. The first
female figure whom Christy will encounter as he grows up is
the therapist, Dr Eileen Cole. Inevitably, he falls in love with
her. Dr Cole is coded throughout the film as the classic be-
trayer, her tight, expensive clothing and short cut hair suggesting castration in comparison with which Mary Carr,
somewhat plump and in loose-fitting nurse's clothing, is
lover-as-mother. In a set-piece fraught with humiliation,

Christy tells Dr Cole that he loves her at the dinner following his first painting exhibition. She has already noticed that
he has been drinking heavily and warns him to "Take it
easy." Christy responds, "You're not my mother, never forget that." Similarly, at the launch of his book, Mary says to
him, "Don't think I'm your mother, just because I'm looking
after you for the evening," to which he replies, "I don't need
a fucking psychology lesson."

Christy's father, Mr Brown (Ray McAnally) is a bricklayer
who, during the course of the film, is laid off. He is gruff and
authoritarian, asserting his right to "be obeyed in my own
house" whilst remaining unaware that the real control in the
family lies with his wife. In terms of the film's diegesis (fictional construction), Mr Brown has little or no agency and
events unfold largely outside of his influence. As the initial
flashbacks represent him, he is a man teetering on the brink
of dispossession, his impending powerlessness shored off
through excessive displays of atavistic (but, in the film's vision, endearing) masculinity. Not only is he unreasonable, he
is ill educated, unable to solve his daughter's primary school
arithmetic problem (another invented sequence). The young
Christy (Hugh O'Conor) who is lying on the floor as his father dismissively pronounces that there is no such thing as a
quarter of a quarter, since a quarter *is* a quarter, makes his
first attempt to indicate that he has solved the problem by
gripping the chalk between his toes and writing on the
blackboard. On this occasion, his family is unable to make
sense of his communication and he continues to be viewed
as mentally as well as physically handicapped.

These early scenes establish *My Left Foot*'s world as one
that is parochial and largely unenlightened. The maternity
ward in which Christy is born is an almost surreal space, the
curtains around each bed suggesting isolation and joyless-
ness. After he has been informed of his son's disability, Mr
Brown repairs to the pub where his neighbours jeer him,

predicting that this will be the end of the (paternal) line for him. Unable to afford the price of a pint, Mr Brown is reduced to taking a swing at one of the drinkers before repairing home. The Brown household is represented as a sanctuary from the outside world where neighbours pass cruel remarks about the young Christy who, for want of anything better, is pushed around in an old boxcar. The religious authorities are little better and when Mrs Brown takes Christy with her to Church, the priest intones to him: "You know that you can never get out of hell. You can get out of purgatory but you can never get out of hell."

Christy is indeed locked into hell and it is his attempts to break out of it that constitute the film's dynamic. They also mark the dialogue between past and present, personified in Christy's desire to achieve manhood whilst rejecting his father's ways. His pre-oedipal state is brought to a close when he demonstrates, in one of the film's most moving set-pieces, that he can understand speech and communicate an advanced intelligence by writing with his left foot on a slate. Now, his family can read his first written word, M-O-T-H-E-R. Instantly, Mr Brown scoops him up, gleefully shouting, "He's a Brown!" and takes him off to the pub, his initiation into the world of men.

The remedial help Christy needs is put beyond the resources of the Brown family as a consequence of their father's unemployment ("a brick hit the foreman on the head accidentally on purpose"). Despite this, and the fact that the family are reduced to a pauper's lifestyle, subsisting on bowls of porridge, Mrs Brown is quietly spiriting away small amounts of cash in order to purchase Christy a wheelchair. In another set-piece, this fact emerges and Mr Brown is outraged. By this stage, the resourceful Christy has staged a daylight robbery on a coal delivery cart and, with the assistance of his brothers, provided the family with illicit heat. Aware that his patriarchal control is being eroded by a combination of his own powerlessness and his son's intellectual superiority, Mr Brown appears increasingly redundant within the family configuration.

One final incident illustrates the intransigence of the old ways that Mr Brown represents. Informed by his wife that their daughter is marrying out of necessity, he tears into mother and child, cursing them for being "the ould woman who lives in a shoe and the daughter who couldn't keep her knickers on".

In contrast, Christy expresses himself through painting and learns to speak by repeating passages from Shakespeare (a reference, perhaps, to Daniel Day-Lewis's well-known stage career since, again, this is a departure from the original book). However, when these outlets fail him and he is tortured by sexual frustration, he retreats into the world of his father, drinking heavily and swearing at all who try to help him. The old order lurks not far below the surface of the new, causing his mother to comment: "You get more like your father every day: all hard on the outside, all putty on the inside."

Christy can only break the cycle by turning his back on his father's tradition of manual labour. He is able to substitute himself for his father almost immediately after the latter's death when he receives the money, £800, for his book. Mrs Brown is overwhelmed by this, "Eight hundred pound [*sic*]. That's more than your poor father earned in a whole year." This is just one of a number of overt comparisons made between Mr Brown's struggle to support the family financially as a labourer and the adult Christy's access to "easy money" through his artistic skills. Whilst *My Left Foot* may not embrace progress unambiguously, it does make it quite clear that Christy is able to find a way to break free of his real as well as his symbolic entrapment and in a manner which may even be considered a parallel for Sheridan's personal trajectory (through making money out of his art). Not

only does Christy's escape from working-class poverty mirror Sheridan's own career; it speaks directly to Ireland in
the late 1980s. To a much greater extent indeed than in the
1930s, the manual labouring classes had been forced to
adapt to new work practices or lose out; intellectual capital
was increasingly replacing industrial capabilities.

Christy's movement away from the background represented by his father, and his liberation from the category of
"mental defective" assigned to him by society, are articulated
through the film's increasing spatial as well as temporal evolution. Christy moves from his home, to the streets, to the
pub, to the art gallery and eventually to the reading at the
stately home of Lord Castlewelland (Cyril Cusack). This
progress upwards and outwards is summarised in the sequence in which Christy's family is brought from their inner-
city home by a cortege of limousines, through the iconic
Dublin landscape, to the mansion where Christy, in tuxedo,
will perform. The closing moments take Christy even further
from his origins as he and Mary Carr toast each other at
what could only be described as a tourist's-eye-view of Dublin — looking down over the Joyce (Martello) Tower from
Killiney Hill on the salubrious Southside, now so beloved of
celebrities seeking a Dublin address.

"Looks can be deceiving. It's a bit sentimental," Christy
warns Mary Carr early on about his book. Given the subject
matter, *My Left Foot*, the film, is not, in fact, overly sentimental. A restrained soundtrack (by Elmer Bernstein) avoids the
temptation indulged in by so many Irish films of re-arranging
lachrymose Irish folk tunes. The orchestration only comes to
the fore in moments of triumph, providing an upbeat, almost
tribal sound that recalls Irish dance music, although without
over-emphasis. This celebratory use of Irish dance music may
be accredited to the musical co-ordinator, Bill Whelan, who
was soon to make his name as composer of the soundtrack
to *Riverdance*. Ambivalent as it is about the past, *My Left Foot*

reserves its sentimentality for its depiction of Mrs Brown. As
the shot of father and son lying head-to-head on the ground
after Mr Brown's death suggests, both share the same fatal
flaws, of violence and irrationality. Mrs Brown, in contrast, is
a monument to probity. She is the eternal mother, the peasant woman as child bearer whose very lack of sophistication
underpins her continuity with an archaic past.

This sense of the eternal is reinforced by the film's refusal to anchor its plot in any one time. Whilst we are informed that *My Left Foot* starts with Christy's birth in 1932,
there is little to tie it in to a particular period. The Second
World War (or the "Emergency") takes place during the
course of the story but the script contains no references to
it. The contrast is simply one between the primitive and the
modern, between an Ireland of the past stuck in its rituals of
drink and childbirth, fighting and sentiment, and the Ireland
of the present, symbolised by champagne and worldly success. Even this, the film regards with some equivocation. The
celebrations held to mark Christy's first exhibition are
marred by the character's drunken declaration of love for
Dr Cole (discussed above); the middle-class art lovers are
viewed with some contempt and the audience is encouraged
to share Mrs Brown's reservations about her son's abandonment of the family group in favour of a night out with his
new circle of "friends". Both of Christy's parents have already signalled their concern over his aspirations, symbolised by his fervent embrace of Shakespeare, and the film
appears to sympathise with their point of view. Yet, at the
same time, money and success offer Christy a way out of his
emotional imprisonment.

Sheridan, too, was to enjoy the same celebrity status
with the success, particularly in the US, of *My Left Foot*. The
film secured five nominations for the Academy Awards in
1990 for: Best Film, Best Director, Best Actor, Best Supporting Actress and Best Adapted Screenplay. Its main competi-

tion came from Oliver Stone's *Born on the Fourth of July* (US, 1989), Peter Weir's *Dead Poets Society* (US, 1989), Bruce Beresford's *Driving Miss Daisy* (US, 1989) and Phil Alden Robinson's *Field of Dreams* (US, 1989). At the risk of generalising, it would seem that the so-called "feel good factor" was decisive in securing nominations that year. As the world economy took a downturn, so films such as *My Left Foot* offered the reassurance that the individual could triumph over adversity. Thus, the latter three films incorporated sentimental tales of ageing and the generation gap into their celebration of selfhood, whilst *Born on the Fourth of July* integrated an angry tirade against official failure to recognise the sacrifices made by the Vietnam generation into its own "disability" storyline. Ultimately, Sheridan's film won two Academy Awards, for Best Actor and Best Supporting Actress.

My Left Foot only enjoyed a minimal release in the UK, a failure generally accredited to its distributor, Palace Pictures. Even before the Academy Awards had been announced, it had become available on video, thus denying it further life as a theatrical release. In the crucial US market, however, its distributors, Miramax, opened the film in just two cinemas and gambled on positive reviews and word of mouth. Much of the film's success is accredited to a review by the influential critic of *The New Yorker*, Pauline Kael, written from the New York Film Festival of autumn 1989. "Right from the first shot, it's clear that the Irish playwright-director Jim Sheridan . . . knows what he's doing . . ." she enthused, adding, in an extended article, that "Day-Lewis seizes the viewer; he takes possession of you. His interpretation recalls Olivier's crookbacked, long-nosed Richard III; Day-Lewis's Christy Brown has the sexual seductiveness that was so startling in the Olivier Richard." She interpreted the story as "a whirling satire of the Irishman as impetuous carnal dreamer" and concluded that "This great, exhilarating movie

— a comedy about suffering — gives him [Christy Brown]
new life as a legendary Irish hero" (Kael, 1989: 98, 99, 100).

Other critics were equally upbeat, praising the film for
its lack of sentimentality, the actors' skills and Sheridan's
direction. Once audience figures showed that the film was
taking off, it was gradually opened in other cinemas nation-
wide, ultimately taking $14.7 million on a production cost of
$3 million, making it the tenth most profitable US release of
the year (Klady, 1991: 11). In Ireland, *My Left Foot* was en-
thusiastically reviewed. *The Irish Times* greeted it as "a mar-
vellously performed and wholly compelling film" (Dwyer,
1989: 12). *The Sunday Tribune* considered Sheridan's debut to
be, "a thoroughly accomplished movie that not only seems
likely to get its money back but deserves to be a critical success as well" (Carty, 1989: 19). Other critics agreed, many
seeing it to be as much Pearson's as Sheridan's achievement.

The recognition gained by *My Left Foot* overseas was to
be a key factor in turning the tide in favour of the establishment of an Irish film industry. Historically, the Irish government policy had engaged in a two-pronged policy towards
film, of active discouragement of the evolution of a film culture (through censorship) on the one hand, and through
their failure, on the other, to establish the structures necessary to support an indigenous industry. When Noel Pearson
first sought financing for *My Left Foot*, no funding was forthcoming from Irish sources. Nor was he able to obtain backing from Hollywood financiers for a film with an unknown
director. It was only when Daniel Day-Lewis agreed to take
the role of Christy that Granada Television provided the
major part (the reports conflict, but the sum seems to have
been around 65 per cent) of the film's budget. The production's financial and critical success led to open public debate
as to the potential of the Irish film industry, particularly
given the fact that Granada stood to benefit considerably
from profits on its investment. Charles Haughey's prevarica-

tion on the *Gay Byrne Show* was an early indication of his continuing refusal to re-establish the Film Board; ironically, it may have been *My Left Foot*'s very success that led him to argue for the adequacy of private and commercial funding of Irish films.

It was not until the new Labour/Fianna Fáil coalition came into power that the Taoiseach, Albert Reynolds, announced the establishment of a special working group on the film production industry at the opening, in 1992, of the Irish Film Centre in Dublin's Temple Bar district. The ensuing report noted that:

> The Group is mindful of the fact that — to take Australia as just one example — the success of a country's film industry can have a profound positive effect on international opinion towards that country, with unquantifiable but real benefits accruing to it. In the Irish context, the degree of success of films such as *My Left Foot*, *The Field*, *The Dead*, *The Commitments*, *Hear My Song*, *Far and Away* and *Into the West* is not dissimilar in overall quantity/numbers to the experience in Australia say 10 years ago — a successful trend which has, since then, placed Australian film-making squarely and confidently in the international arena. (Special Working Group on the Film Production Industry, 1992: 29)

The Report, however, worried that this mini-boom might now be over and that the time had come to initiate more effective measures that would place the nascent Irish film industry on a more stable footing. In fact, if we look at this list of films more closely, only one Irish director — Jim Sheridan — was involved in their making; none was financed by Irish investment or distributed by Irish distributors. Thus, all their profits (probably not an issue in the case of *Far and Away*!) were repatriated to their financial country of origin.

Indeed, what may have appeared to the authors of the report as evidence of an emerging Irish film industry could equally be described as the labours of two Irish Americans — John Huston and Ron Howard, directors of *The Dead* (Huston, US/UK, 1987) and *Far And Away* (Howard, US, 1992) respectively — an assortment of British filmmakers, and Jim Sheridan.

Following the publication of the Special Working Group's report, the Labour Minister in the newly created Department of Arts, Culture and the Gaeltacht, Michael D. Higgins, presided over the implementation of a series of measures designed to aid the establishment of an Irish film industry. In 1993, the Irish Film Board was re-activated and adjustments were made to Section 35 (now Section 481) tax relief to make the scheme more attractive to corporate investors whilst also providing opportunities for individual investors. In the same year, the Broadcasting Authority (Amendment) Bill required RTÉ (the national broadcaster) to make specific amounts of money available to the independent production sector to produce television programmes (although these were not necessarily feature films).

Clearly, Sheridan's success in the overseas market was as crucial as the reception of his films at home to provoking the government into supporting film production. The significance of *My Left Foot* was that it demonstrated that international audiences would watch Irish films if they were structured around universal themes and conformed to a recognised model of filmmaking; in other words, if they looked like Hollywood cinema. This in itself has not been unproblematic and, as has already been suggested in the preface to this book, may well account for some reluctance on the part of the academic establishment to accord his films the same critical favour as they did his immediate predecessors, the low-budget, avant-garde filmmakers of the mid-1970s onwards.

Despite the fact that a British television channel financed it, *My Left Foot* is now associated with Ireland's entry into a global filmmaking market that is synonymous with Hollywood product. In common with other industries, this market is influenced less by national borders than by regional advantage. Production practices follow competing economic incentives across the globe, with low-cost, efficient labour, tax breaks and an up-to-the-moment communications infrastructure dictating the desirability of any one location. Small countries cannot hope to go it alone in this environment, and must stake their claims for a slice of multinational funding in order to establish their own production base. At the same time, they must advertise their attractiveness as a location for non-indigenous productions. In cultural terms, the mobilisation of global capital by what is now seen to be a "culture industry" has been viewed with extreme anxiety; there is a sense that, in the race to please the international consumer, the specificities of history and geography are being abandoned. For many, the success of *Riverdance* epitomises the obeisance of Irish culture to the lure of the dollar, the yen or the lira. *My Left Foot* is central to this debate, since it established a template for employing international finance to support an Irish commercial cinema. Martin McLoone reminds us that:

> The success of *My Left Foot* was seen at the time as vindication of the government's strategy of favouring the commercial sector but, as many observers argued, there is a price to pay for this type of financing. While Sheridan's film is by no means the worst offender, the fact remains that such financing inevitably involves compromises in the style and theme of the films. The danger is that, to attract financial support, such films propose a view of Ireland that is already familiar to international funders and which funders in turn believe audiences are likely to recognise and

identify with. Ultimately, they offer conservative images of Ireland that do not challenge existing cinematic traditions. (McLoone, 2000: 114–15)

Such an argument, whilst containing much truth, lays itself
open to charges of essentialism on the one hand, and academic elitism on the other. For a start, it is simply not prac-
ticable to imagine that Irish films can be completed without
international financing. Film is one of the most costly of artistic media, and even a low-budget work won't see change
out of half a million euro. That level of finance is not available from Irish sources alone; moreover, it has been consistently demonstrated that the kind of government subsidies
that would free a production from the need to seek overseas' investors are no guarantee of high-quality films. Even
the much-acclaimed independent, avant-garde films of the
1970s and early 1980s were reliant on outside money, usually British. So the dream of a pure Irish cinema must remain
just that. Taking the argument further, a film that McLoone
and many others greeted as one of the most subversive and
artistically accomplished of recent times, Neil Jordan's *The
Butcher Boy*, was largely financed by an American studio
(Warner Brothers). Most producers would agree with Noel
Pearson when he comments that:

> it's so hard to get the Americans to invest at the
> script stage here, fairly decent money, that the prob-
> lem for us with an Irish film, before they'll put in
> what they think is reasonable money, which is $5
> million upwards, they want names, even if the names
> don't fit the parts. The trick for the producer is to
> resist that and protect the script and the director,
> and walking the tight line between what's really good
> for the film and at the same time what's going to
> guarantee it a release in the States. Because, no mat-
> ter what they tell you, success in America largely de-

termines success in the rest of the world. (Pearson,
1998: 18)

Ultimately, the argument is more about quality than funding.
In this highly subjective arena, art films, particularly those
from the European tradition of filmmaking, tend to be more
highly valued. Art cinema is driven less by the working
through of dramatic events than by the exploration of sub-
jectivity. The "happy ending", long the staple of Hollywood
filmmaking practices, is shunned by the art film as escapist
and improbable. Art films tend to be culturally specific in
contrast to the universality of Hollywood.

The paradigm shifts as generalisations are abandoned.
There is no doubt that neither *My Left Foot* nor any of Sheridan's subsequent films are endowed with the same aesthetic
qualities as, for example, the films of Neil Jordan. Sheridan's
ability to tell a story through dialogue and performance has
always taken precedence over his sense of the visual. Furthermore, he has deliberately situated himself within the
populist tradition:

> The tradition of great stories in the world is gener-
> ally literate and has come down to us through
> scribes, from *Oedipus the King* to *The Playboy of the
> Western World*. It is on these texts that criticism and
> analysis is based, from Aristotle to T.S. Eliot. There
> is another world of story telling however, in fairy
> tales and folk myths that were orally transmitted and
> came down by firelight and have a ruptured history.

> Film in most cases belongs to this stock, best mani-
> fested by the seanchaí in Ireland. These are myth
> stories, usually with happy endings. It makes absolute
> sense for an old Hollywood mogul to say, "Tell me
> the story." He listens and reacts on a primal level,
> not an intellectual one. Surely that is the way the old
> fairy and folk tales developed; by repetition, seeing

which bits worked, keeping them and polishing them.
This is not necessarily condescending to a listener,
for the tellers or listeners worried little about why
the stories worked, they were just glad they did.
They performed the kind of function that modern
analysis performs, of speaking about the unspeakable
in an acceptable way. The story tellers were telling
tales that connected at a primal level and for me that
is what the best films do. (Sheridan, 1989: 12)

My Left Foot is undeniably commercial in its orientation. It
contains recognisable, stereotypical figures, is easy to follow,
swiftly paced, has a classical structure and an upbeat ending.
Its reception by Irish audiences suggests, however, that it
addressed them in a culturally specific manner. Even with its
concessions to a mainstream, overseas audience, the film is
recognisably Irish. Its characters, dialogue and humour are
drawn from a tradition that is both literary and oral — perhaps best seen in the work of Roddy Doyle, another populist, commercial success who has fallen foul of the "purist"
strain of criticism. It established the partnership of Pearson
and Sheridan as commercially viable and, by extension, the
Irish film industry as culturally valid. The challenge of maintaining a reasonable balance between local culture and history and global expectations has been a consistent element
of Jim Sheridan's filmmaking career. As we shall see, in the
next chapter, his depiction of a darker, more violent and
regressive Ireland, in *The Field,* was to teach him that this
view of Ireland might strike a chord with local audiences but
held little attraction for the American market that would
decide the financial success of his work.

Chapter Two

The Field (1990): Revising History

In my interview with him, Sheridan remarks that many people like *The Field* the best of all his films (see interview). It seemed to surprise him, though perhaps it should not. Made in 1989 and released in 1990, *The Field* is an epic narrative of life in the west of Ireland during the inter-war period. As I will be arguing in this chapter, it is a work that offers a more complex hero than is common in Sheridan's films, and with its ambiguous attitude to the past, one that reflects the strong sense of crisis in historical representation that characterised Irish society in the period in which it was made.

The story of *The Field* revolves around the Bull McCabe's (Richard Harris) struggle to buy the eponymous field from the Widow (Frances Tomelty). His competitor for the purchase is the Irish-American, the Yank (Tom Berenger), who has returned from the United States and plans to develop the area. The Bull McCabe has not spoken to his wife (Brenda Fricker) for 18 years and is haunted by the death (by suicide) of their elder son Seamie. Meanwhile, their younger son Tadgh (Sean Bean) can do no right; abetted by "the Bird" O'Donnell (John Hurt), he tries to scare away the Widow. When the Bull forces him to fight the Yank, Tadgh is not up to it and the Bull ends up killing the Yank himself. Tadgh falls in love with the Tinker Girl (Jenny Conroy),

something his father opposes, as she will not bring with her
a dowry of land. In the end, Tadgh dies trying to save the
cattle his father is driving into the sea in a fit of madness and
the film closes with the Bull wading, ranting, into the waves.

   The Field is an adaptation of the John B. Keane play of the
same name. As with *My Left Foot*, Sheridan, writing on his
own this time, made free with the originating text. The film
is now set in the 1930s (though critics have mistaken it for
the 1940s) rather than the 1960s of the play. Keane is a
well-known publican and often comic dramatist of local
Kerry life, but the production almost entirely dispenses with
the pub setting and its colourful patrons, moving the action
between the Bull McCabe's cottage and the boglands around
Leenane in Connemara. Gone therefore is the publican's
wife, the disenchanted Maimie Flanagan, who articulates
much of the play's critique of small-town Irish life in the
1960s:

> If you get your hair done different they whisper about
> you. Dress up in a bit of style and they stare at you.
> You'd want an armoured car if you wore a pair of
> slacks. Do you know how long it is since he [her hus-
> band, Mick Flanagan] had a bath? A year! Imagine, a
> whole year! He changes his shirt every Sunday and
> sleeps in it for the rest of the week. (Keane, 1991: 16)

Gone too is Leamy, her son, who must decide at the play's
end whether to collude in the communal silence over the
outsider's death, and thus perpetuate the archaic value system that governs Carraigthomond, or share his knowledge
with the police and in doing so become that classic Irish villain, the informer.

   The outsider, whose desire to purchase the plot of land
which the Bull McCabe considers his own and who thus ac-
tivates the drama, becomes an Irish-American, the Yank. In
Keane's original, he is an Irishman who plans to return from

England to placate his wife and repeat his business success in Ireland. Crucially, Keane's construction of the pivotal character of the Bull makes him more a mealy-mouthed bully in league with his conniving son than the towering patriarch of Sheridan's adaptation. Keane further accentuates the stand-off between the Bull and the police so that the play's thematic thrust is an interrogation of the lawlessness of rural Ireland. Kevin Rockett has been critical of these alterations, arguing that Sheridan has discarded "the film's potential for exploring Ireland during one of its most crucial conjunctures when it was changing from an inward-looking to an outward-looking society" (Rockett, 1994: 139) and suggests that this was done to satisfy foreign backers in search of the kind of pastoralism that traditional representations of Irishness provided. Rockett further surmises that the substitution of the Yank for the character of William Dee was a response to the exigencies of co-production finance (ibid.).

Disputes over what period *The Field* is, or ought to be, set in is to miss the point that this film, even more than *My Left Foot* did, aspires to the mythic and, therefore, the time-less. The work's indifference to current affairs, its neglect of the kind of period effect — branded goods, details of design, musical cues — that in cinema signifies the recreation of a particular moment in the past, are symptomatic of its deliberate lack of historical specificity. Nor is its vision of the past one of nostalgic pastoralism; where it does engage with life in Ireland in the 1930s, the picture it paints is of a country that is mired in the myths of the past. This, as I will be arguing, is a film about myth, and in particular its place within Irish culture.

Central to this theme is the film's portrayal of the Bull McCabe. The part had initially been written with Ray McAnally in mind but, after McAnnally's premature death, Richard Harris took the role. Harris, from Limerick, is himself a larger-than-life personality. Before his appearance in

The Field, he had been absent from any notable cinema productions for over ten years and had spent the intervening
time touring in a theatrical production of *Camelot*, a version
of the King Arthur legend in which he had taken the part of
Arthur. His performance in Sheridan's film exudes theatrical-
ity and recalls Daniel Day-Lewis's tour-de-force in *My Left
Foot* (Harris was nominated for an Oscar but was unsuccessful). Indeed, this role was to return Harris to the screen acting limelight and he subsequently took a series of major
parts in films including that of English Bob in *Unforgiven* (Clint
Eastwood, US, 1992) and Marcus Aurelius in *Gladiator* (Ri-
dley Scott, US, 2000). His physical appearance in *The Field*,
with burning eyes and long, flowing beard suggests Renais-
sance interpretations of Old Testament figures — Moses,
Abraham or even the Almighty. His sons, one dead, the
other surviving, are Cain and Abel, Isaac or Christ, symbolic
victims of ancestral grievances, reluctantly yoked to historical destiny. Then again, he is King Lear, his obsession with
inheritance pushing him eventually into madness, or Yeats's
Cuchulainn, fighting the ungovernable tide.

In an Irish context, the invocation of myth as part of the
historicising project has been a particularly contentious
strategy. If the revivalists believed that the reanimation of
the great mythic heroes of Ireland's past — Cuchulainn, Finn
Mac Cool, Oisín — would instil pride in the nationalist
movement, so a new generation of historians of the 1930s
led by Theodore Moody and Robert Dudley Edwards argued
that the recourse to myth inhibited a true understanding of
history. Historical writing was to be freed from emotional
and personal interpretation and subjected to rigorous standards of empirical research. This in turn would lead to a re-
interpretation of the Irish Republican tradition (Brady, 1994:
3–31). The response, to void historical discourse of its romantic excess, was deemed by many to produce an arid

methodology that was no more justifiable than that which it sought to replace.

The outbreak of violence in Northern Ireland led many historians to question the effects of perpetuating the old rhetoric, in particular the idealisation of blood sacrifice and the ancient warrior codes of Cuchulainn. The suggestion that present-day paramilitaries were able to justify their activities through recourse to these ideals lay at the heart of such anxieties. It was not, however, just the situation within Northern Ireland that encouraged revisionists to re-assess previous versions of Irish history but:

> the unexpected re-examination of Irish identity that followed upon Ireland's sudden encounter with Europe to the collapse of consensus in the light of successive governments' inability to resolve the Republic's chronic social and economic problems. (Brady, 1994: 23)

To this we can also add the new accessibility of historical documents from the British archives and the publication of the secret Dáil debates on the Treaty (Laffan, 1991: 110). The burgeoning debate was given a shot in the arm by the publication of Ruth Dudley Edwards's provocatively entitled biography of Patrick Pearse, *Patrick Pearse, The Triumph of Failure* in 1977 and Roy Foster's *Modern Ireland* in 1988. The question of how to commemorate the Easter Rising of 1916 threw what could otherwise have been an arcane academic affair into the public domain as both sides took to the airwaves in what became an increasingly personal debate about whether the deconstruction of the myth of Republicanism was ultimately unpatriotic. The tone of the anti-revisionist camp might be summarised by Desmond Fennell's contention that the Irish people traditionally:

saw the nation represented by great men, women
and movements, righteous insurgents, and brave soldiers, inspired by right ideas and acting rightly. They
saw this with pride. They cherished songs, poems
and other writings emanating from this inheritance,
and they revered countless places, buildings and relics which it had imbued with value. The revisionist
historian, instead of maintaining this framework of
meaning, moral interpretation, and anchored value,
and renewing it through industrious and creative re-
vision, set about demolishing it. Their articles, books,
radio talks and speeches represented the Irish nationalist tradition, and in particular its revolution, as
radically flawed by wrong ideas and wrong action, to
such a degree as to make it something we should be
ashamed of. "Forget," they told the Irish and the
world of Africa and Asia, America and Europe, "that
you saw in the Irish Revolution one of the great lib-
erating landmarks of this century and treasured the
names of MacSwiney and de Valera. It was all a mistake, a huge blunder, something we should not have
done, or at least not that way." (Fennell, 1994: 189)

A more measured response to the revisionists' claims can be
found in the writings of Brendan Bradshaw who contended
that the "value-free" approach to history espoused by the
revisionists was simply "value-based interpretation in another guise" (Bradshaw, 1994: 201). He argued that their
approach to history was based on evasion (the neglect of
key moments in Irish history) and suppression (of the
trauma of events such as the Famine). In order to downplay
the progression of Nationalism through the ages up until the
present, the revisionists had therefore stressed the disconti-
nuities of Irish history rather than exploring its holistic nature. The revisionists were generally accused of draining
Irish history not just of its populism but also of its energy;
they were accused of being overly dry and elitist.

A further aspect of contemporary Irish society has been its willed embrace of historical oblivion; history has become meaningless other than as a commodity. This is not just a response to being beaten over the head with history of whatever hue, but is simply an inevitable consequence of belonging to the culture of post-modernity. The past, its rough edges erased, has become an object for sale, of particular use to a country heavily dependent on tourism. Its historical events and iconic figures have been sold on tea towels and mocked on satirical shows. For Eric Hobsbawm, lamenting the death of historical memory:

> The destruction of the past, or rather of the social mechanisms that link one's contemporary experience to that of earlier generations, is one of the most characteristic and eerie phenomena of the late twentieth century. Most young men and women at the century's end grow up in a sort of permanent present lacking any organic relation to the public past of the times they live in. (Hobsbawm, 1994: 3)

We can thus see Sheridan's *The Field* as a conscious intervention in a public arena unsure over how to remember its past. At first glance, it seems on multiple occasions to have as its mission the retrieval of a romantic view of history from the clutches of dull historicism. With its emphasis on land and dispossession, it echoes the great themes of Irish agrarian rebellion, specifically the right to own, work and sell one's own property. The vehicle for this discourse is the Bull McCabe and it is through him that *The Field* articulates a mode of historical interpretation that would not have seemed out of place in the national schools of the 1930s. "This is what we would be without the land, boy," he says to Tadgh, in an establishing scene, blowing away dandelion seed. The analogy, that without land, the Irish are both barren and dispersed, is followed through with the information that the Bull's brothers and sisters were forced to emigrate and that Seamie (whose invention is another major departure from the original) died because the Bull had said that there was "only living in the land for one".

The field of the title is endowed with multiple meanings and associations. It is both the symbol of hope, the future, and a reminder of the hardships of the past. Its vivid emerald green distinguishes it from the ill-tended fields surrounding it, suggesting that it is an enclave of purity surrounded by mediocrity, not merely a personal symbol but a national one. It is Ireland as a historically contested space, the "real" Ireland, located in the Celtic West and threatened by hostile modernity (the Yank). The Bull calls it "my child" and remembers how "our fathers' fathers' fathers' father built those walls, dug that soil with their bare hands, and our souls is [sic] buried down there; and your [Tadgh's] sons' sons' sons will take care of it, boy." It is, literally, the motherland, referred to as "she" by the Bull, and a symbol of the triumph of the Republic — when reminded that the English are gone, the Bull responds, "Gone, because I drove them out, me and my kind, Flanagan. Gone but not forgotten."

Through his rhetoric, the Bull establishes himself simultaneously as the bearer of history and its victim; if at first glance the villains of his piece are the British, the usurpers of the land, a secondary discourse reminds us that he has been failed as much by the present as by the past. The Bull may be the product of centuries of dispossession but he is also enchained by an inert society that has failed to transform itself into the nation imagined by the visionaries that formulated independence. A Free State it may now be, but under its surface hides a thinly submerged feudal structure, where ownership of the land lies not with the peasantry but with the new Catholic bourgeoisie (the Widow), and its guarantor (the Church). This node of power, the Bull rightly sees as dating back to the Famine: "No priest died at the time of

the Famine, only poor people like us." Where Keane's original play pivots around a central concern that rural Ireland is
bound by a set of laws that are best seen as representing an
atavistic value system at odds with contemporary notions of
the legal, in Sheridan's version of events, this message is
somewhat opaque. Certainly, the film sees history not as
linear, but as circular and repetitive. It rejects the humanist
notion that we are progressing along a great path of enlight-
ened discovery, learning from our errors and striving for a
better future. In Sheridan's world, both older and younger
generations are trapped in time and in a cycle of violence.

The Field is structured to reflect this theme. It ends as it
began, with the sea. In the opening sequences, a donkey's
corpse is glimpsed falling through murky water, its teeth
bared in a mocking grin; this animal we will discover be-
longed to the Tinkers (Travellers) and was killed by Tadgh.
They will spend the film demanding their "blood money" in
compensation. Water continues to be associated with death
throughout. In a dramatic set-piece, the Bull, Tadgh and the
Yank meet in darkness at the waterfall to sort out their differences and, at the water's edge, the Bull beats the Yank to
death. Framed by the cascade, the Bull falls to his knees under the moonlight and prays to the Lord for forgiveness.
Finally, Tadgh is run over the cliff to his death by his father's
stampeding cattle and the Bull wades out into the sea, bran-
dishing his staff at the waves and cursing his fate. Lear or
Canute, he can control his destiny no more than he can control that of his sons. In a final moment of insight amidst his
madness, he realises that he is caught in a cycle of inheritance and dispossession, crying out, "Damn my father and
my mother for slaving me to the accursed famine field and
breaking me for it." The film has animated a great mythic
hero, only to condemn him to madness and death. Perhaps,
the time in which he found himself was not worthy of he-

roes, or perhaps the heroes were all wrong, mythic figures trapped in a pedestrian society.

In the same vein, given his unstable vantage-point, the Bull's analysis that the poverty of his life is the culmination of centuries of colonial dispossession must also be questioned. Sentiments such as his echo a narrow, nationalist interpretation of history. Yet *The Field* stops short of wholeheartedly indicting the inheritors of the republican/nationalist mantle. What forces are preventing the Bull from realising his dream? Why do the villagers offer so little resistance to his lethal conspiracies? Why has Irish rural society of the 1930s remained so disenfranchised, well beyond independence?

The answer, which the film never fully articulates, is that independence has brought with it little change. In this context, David Lloyd has noted that:

> One of the earliest post-colonial nations, Ireland has largely conformed to the model of bourgeois nationalism that Frantz Fanon analysed — presciently for other newly independent nations — in *The Wretched of the Earth*. The adoption, virtually wholesale, of the state institutions of the colonizing power, and conformity to its models of representative democracy, poses what Fanon terms the "sterile formalism" of bourgeois politics against the popular movements its institutions are designed to contain. The state, which represents the point of intersection of the nation with the unilaterally defined universality of the world economic order, becomes an effective brake on the decolonizing process culturally as well as economically. (Lloyd, 1993: 7)

The film's refusal to anchor itself more convincingly in the era in which it is ostensibly set may indeed enhance its dialogue with myth but it militates against the achievement of any specific critique of post-independence nationalism. The absence of any mention of independence, the Civil War, partition, or de Valera leaves it devoid of points of reference. The State, or its representatives, other than the Priest, do not figure. Again, although the Yank, with his ambitions to harness the local river for hydro-electricity and build roads across the countryside, obviously symbolises the arrival of neo-colonialism and multi-national companies, for the Bull all he represents are those Irish who fled during the Famine: "When the going got tough, they ran away to America, they ran away from the Famine, but we stayed. You went to America to make your few dollars and then you think you can buy the land." Here the film most obviously displays the disjuncture between itself and its originating text. As Rockett (above) has argued, anxieties about the transformation of rural Ireland into a vast building site designed to supply the needs of overseas corporations belong more properly in a tale set in the 1960s.

Sheridan's remark that "*The Field* is only about the past in so much as it's probably really about the IRA and nationalism and what it all means. For me it's not really about the past" (see interview) indicates that it was indeed his intention that his film should provide an overt critique of nationalist orthodoxies, both historically and as they continued into the present. How much this was understood at the time of the film's release is debatable. The key to any reading of the production is how we interpret the figure of the Bull McCabe.

Suggestions of personality differences between Harris and Sheridan accompanied the making and release of *The Field* and may account for their conflicting understandings of the role. As Sheridan says:

> I wanted him [the Bull] to be less sympathetic than
> Richard wanted him to be. That was an argument
> between us. And that comes over when the plot

point turns in the first act. I think Richard thought
that when he gives out to the Priest and the American that you suddenly see his reason for it. And I
only wanted to see his mania. I wanted that moment
when you know you are in the control of a psychopath. (see interview)

Even outside of Harris's performance, the film invites the
viewer to feel a certain level of sympathy for the Bull's
grievance. As a number of overhead shots indicate, his field
is indeed much better tended than any of the surrounding
ones and logic would dictate that his care of it has added to
its worth. Equally, he is consistently depicted as a man of
honour among a den of thieves. Like the Western hero of
classic cinema, the Bull subscribes to a value system that ele-
vates him above the community of misfits that he must defend. The locals of Carraigthomond are presented as an en-
semble of scabrous, broken-toothed no-goods, entrenched
in an antiquated and misogynistic world-view. A travelling
shot follows the entry of the Widow into the village, the
men, half-hidden behind carts and lurking in the corners of
the pub, leering and catcalling behind her. When she sashays
out of her cottage to pronounce that there is a reserve
price on the field, one of the onlookers throws a lump of
clay at her, causing the Bull to remonstrate to the community at large for their manners, before handing the Widow
up to her cart.

The Bull's son, Tadgh, is himself imbricated in this social
order and an extended sequence shows him and the Bird
blocking the Widow's chimney and hooting at her in the
night. This disgusts the Bull when he hears of it, as does
Tadgh's killing of the tinkers' donkey. Furthermore, at the
end of the film, the Bull's wife drops her silence in order to
exhort him not to break, thus implicitly validating his stance
(in the original, this does not occur).

The film often appears in thrall to the Bull's energies. A key sequence in this regard is the American wake, the dance held to mark the emigration of a family or individual to the United States. The Bull has been dealing with the matchmaker in order to secure a bride for Tadgh. The MacGroarty girl is mooted and meets with the Bull's approval, her hips in particular seeming to promise the continuation of the McCabe lineage. As the dance opens and the music strikes up, the Yank appears, dressed in his usual impeccable clothing. The tinker girl strides around the circle of locals, daring one after another to dance with her. The young men are too intimidated to take up her offer but when the smitten Tadgh looks like he might assent, the Bull steps forward to dance with her whilst simultaneously nudging Tadgh towards the MacGroarty girl. He throws himself into the dance, nimble-footed and energetic, and then relinquishes the tinker girl to the Yank. The rhythms of the Irish tune become increasingly frenetic, in time it seems with the primordial instincts with which the gathering is charged. Tadgh and the Yank move towards each other in threatening gestures and then whirl their partners. As the music gains tempo, a look of panic emerges on the MacGroarty girl's face. Tadgh spins her off her feet and the camera cuts to the Bull, who now tries to stop his son. The dance finally climaxes with the MacGroarty girl collapsing, unconscious, on the boards.

Even after his brutal murder of the Yank, the Bull's abasement to fate and his own peculiar version of religion militate against any real understanding of his pathological nature and, to the end, the audience is positioned so as to feel some sympathy for him.

Most reviews of the production comment on Harris's epic performance as the Bull. Yet, there is a sense that they are so blinded by it, they fail to see that the trajectory of the film is to alienate us from its central character. Thus, for instance, *The Irish Times* review responds sympathetically to the Bull's predicament, noting that:

> The snowballing events that stem from this conflict have serious, far-reaching and tragic consequences; the more the Bull attempts to exert his control, the more he loses control over his land and over himself, and the greater his personal loss accrues.
>
> At the heart of its reflection on tradition, the way the Famine changed Irish life, the attachment to and affection for the land, the suspicion of outsiders and the threat of the new, and the erosion of man-made power bases, the film is uniquely Irish. Yet, although it makes no concession to the international cinema-going audience, it is universal and accessible in its themes and its treatment of them. (Dwyer, 1990: 10)

Dwyer was both right and wrong in his predictions for *The Field*'s reception at home and overseas. The film undoubtedly struck a chord with local audiences, making it the top performing film at the 1990 Irish box office (Myler, 1991: 1–3). We can only speculate as to the reasons for its success, yet it may be, as Dwyer suggests, that, with its appeal to the classic ingredients of Irish drama, it satisfied a desire to revisit old themes within a new context, that of indigenous cinema. It remains impossible to gauge whether its audiences also read it as a critique of romantic nationalism and an indictment of IRA rhetoric.

Overseas critics also greeted the film as embracing familiar Irish themes, but in a manner that veered into derision. Thus, a relatively sympathetic response from the *Guardian* critic considered that:

> There's nothing like playing clichés for all they are worth and it's part of the success of Jim Sheridan's *The Field* that it transcends its awkward moments

> with such conviction . . . Sheridan orchestrates his
> tragedy with such purpose that only occasionally do
> some of his own lines betray him — "Quiet, boy
> quiet," says Harris at one point to his son, "Oi've got
> a terrible rapping in me skull." Such highly coloured
> Oirishry notwithstanding, the film remains at least a
> kind of *tour de force*. And its central performance is
> just that. When the Irish put something on the
> screen, it seems almost to stay there intact and defy
> gravity. (Malcolm, 1991: 27)

His response was echoed by a number of British reviewers
who took some relish in pointing out the "Irishness" of the
film:

> There is no ladling of "Danny Boy" over the sound-
> track of *The Field*. But this new film from writer-
> director Jim Sheridan . . . could not be more Irish if it
> had blarney-stones for teeth and shamrocks growing
> from its ears. (Andrews, 1991: 19)

This critic went on to compare the film with another recent
Irish production:

> After last week's catatonic Emerald Isle opus *Decem-
> ber Bride* [Thaddeus O'Sullivan, UK, 1990], *The Field*
> restores our faith in Ireland's ability to turn simple
> tales into stormy, ragged anthems to the national
> character. (ibid.)

The bizarre aspect of such responses, from an Irish point of
view, is that they are proffered in a positive spirit. (As we
shall see in the next chapter, for truly negative critiques,
Sheridan had to wait for the reaction to *In the Name of the
Father*.) These writers rather liked the film; they simply
equated Irishness with blarney and tempestuousness. Expectations of this sort have obvious consequences for filmmak-

ers hoping to distribute their films in territories other than
Ireland, something they must do in order to render them
financially viable. Such a critical climate also evidently militates against inserting any particularly complex or subversive
themes into a work (as did Thaddeus O'Sullivan in the "cata-
tonic" December Bride). As I shall be arguing below, The Field
can valuably be read as an antidote to the kind of "stage"
Irishness celebrated in John Ford's canonical Irish production, The Quiet Man (Ford, US, 1952). It also adumbrates that
most derided of British films, David Lean's Ryan's Daughter
(Lean, UK, 1970).

Sheridan might have been forewarned. By the time of its
release in the United Kingdom, The Field had already run the
gauntlet of the American press. The Los Angeles Times thun-
dered that:

> The Field, set in Western Ireland in the late '30s, is
> such an impassioned piece of blarney that you can't
> really laugh at it even when it's pulpy and ridiculous
> and wildly over the top. It's an epic-sized howl, and a
> few of the howlers — Richard Harris's patriarchal
> Bull McCabe and John Hurt's half-wit Bird O'Donnell
> — are like black Irish folklore characters brought to
> vivid life. (Rainer, 1990: 11)

A more reasoned New York Times advised its readers that:

> It [The Field] is sincere and symmetrical and full of
> references to primal passions that evoke the tougher
> but less anxious times of long ago. It's a sorrowful
> fable that depends a lot on one's susceptibility to
> sorrowful fables about primal passions. (Canby,
> 1990: 14)

The film's poor performance at the US box office, where it
took just $1,258,057 over a 14-week run, suggests that the
American public were indifferent to such fables (Screen Inter-

national, 1991: 31). More than that, there is a sense that the film's setting, both in time and place, was simply viewed as far-fetched. The critic from the *Village Voice* found comparisons between Christy Brown's physical disability and the Bull's emotional inarticulacy:

> cultural monomania is his cerebral palsy, and that distinction makes this new film by director Jim Sheridan and producer Noel Pearson less universally appealing, more remote, more forbidding. That, and what John Hurt has done to his teeth (Fleischmann, 1991: 62).

In retrospect, it is not surprising that an American audience warmed so little to Sheridan and Pearson's second film. In a country with a brief historical memory (where yesterday is "history"), it is accustomed to a film culture that dresses up history in interesting costumes and furnishes it with charismatic heroes, or retrieves it for nostalgic consumption. Neither could be said of *The Field*. It is also conceivable that the American-Irish constituency cared little to be reminded that this dank, violent landscape was their mother country.

In common with *My Left Foot* and his other films, Sheridan draws on a range of archetypes from other fictional representations of Ireland. This set of references brings with it another history, of symbolic figures. In particular, the Bull's family of silent mother, violent, impotent father, dead son, and rebel son, is constructed in a manner that readily offers itself to an analogous reading. Declan Kiberd, who like Lloyd has mapped Fanon's analyses of postcolonialism onto the history of Ireland in the twentieth century, can thus argue that:

> the patriarchal society of which he was a part would lead the Irish male to strive all the more for control within his own family, if only because of his political

and social impotence outside it. But the evidence of
Irish texts and case-histories would confirm the sus-
picion that the autocratic father is often the weakest
male of all, concealing that weakness under the protective coverage of the prevailing system. . . . Patriarchal values exist in societies where men, lacking
true authority, settle for mere power. (Kiberd, 1996:
390–1)

As we have seen in the previous chapter's discussion of Mrs
Brown, Sheridan's central character is a fusion of the symbolic and the historic. The Bull McCabe's is not just a mythic
presence, but the embodiment of a culture that turns men
into monsters. He has no "true authority"; ultimately he
achieves nothing, and must redouble his efforts to conceal
this by enacting the role of patriarch. Within this configuration, the Bull's wife's silence can be seen as a refutation of
the patriarchal language of violence. The use of Brenda
Fricker in a part that contrasts so sharply with her role in
My Left Foot suggests that the Mother Ireland image has become disengaged from its historical references. She is no
longer the epitome of fertility; instead, she has lost one son
and will have seen the other die by the film's end. Only the
earth is now fertile and that fact will bring little joy to anyone.

On a historical level, her estrangement from her husband recalls the emotional and material deprivations of rural
life in the 1930s. This point is made more forcibly in Keane's
play where the Bull admits to having assaulted his wife over
a dispute about the tinker's pony that she allowed to graze
on the field: "I had a share of booze taken. I walloped her
more than I meant maybe" (Keane, 1991: 55). Indeed, like
the patriarch of _Down All The Days_, the Bull assumes that
beating women is a necessary marital function. When Tadgh,
in the play, complains that the woman he has fixed on to

marry is pampered and headstrong, the Bull's response is, "That will be knocked out of her" (ibid., 56); or, as the tinker girl observes in Sheridan's version, "All fathers beat their children."

Ironically, the Bull is offered a surrogate son, the Yank, for whom the journey back to Ireland is a return to his homeland and the birthplace of his grandfather. At a number of junctures, it is suggested that the Yank and the dead Seamie have become united in the Bull's mind. In one sequence, the camera cuts between the Bull kneeling at the gravestone of his son and the figure of the Yank as he traverses the field in the mist. More explicitly, after the Bull has killed the Yank, he clutches the body to him, reciting, "Thirteen years, six months, twenty-four days," the length of time Seamie has been dead; and again, as the dead man is swung out of the water on a hoist, where he hangs momentarily until he is let down, the Bull calls out, "Seamie!"

Where the protagonist of *My Left Foot* works through his oedipal trajectory and emerges triumphant, the younger generation of *The Field* must all die as a result of the tyrannical father figure. They die not just because he is strong but because they are weak. Most enfeebled is Tadgh, harasser of women, liar and, in his father's eyes, fool. As a representative of the first generation of post-independence Ireland, he is, at best, a regressive figure. The imbalance of power in his relationship with his father is also in part caused by an inequality in actorly presence. Bean, who routinely plays the villain (*Patriot Games* (Philip Noyce, US, 1992), *GoldenEye* (Martin Campbell, UK/US, 1995)), simply does not have the same screen presence as Harris, who outperforms all around him. More than that, however, the Bull represents a patriarchal order, a lineage of violent, lawless men who the film views as magnificent and deplorable in equal measures. He is an anachronism in a world of compromise and indifference, the revenge of history revisited on the present. For as much as the film retrieves, through the Bull, the romantic discourse of nationalism, so it labels it ultimately as destructive.

It is this dimension of the film that marks *The Field* out as Sheridan's most complex work to date. In all his other productions, the central character (generally a young male) is faced with a crisis that he must overcome. This he achieves and the film reaches its resolution. Although the characters played by Daniel Day-Lewis are fascinating for their flaws, their vanity and their anger, they are inevitably set on a narrative path that will lead them to a better understanding of themselves and their surroundings. The films in which they appear leave little room for doubt — we can assume that they will triumph over the odds — and much of their fascination lies at the level of performance. In the Bull, however, we have a true tragic hero. Like King Lear, he will be driven insane, his insistence on pursuing a personal code of honour destroying both his family and himself.

The real conflict within *The Field* is less between the premodern (the Bull) and the modern (the Yank and his reluctant allies, the priest and the police) than between conflicting interpretations of the past and its validity for the present. The elements of the modern are easily removed from the frame; the Yank is killed with a few blows and the priest and police are simply ignored, allowing for the film to work through its real tensions: the ambivalence with which it regards the energy and aggression embodied in the Bull. Unlike many representations of Irish violence, this is not specifically labelled as atavistic but explained in terms of the country's colonial past. As the Bull never tires of articulating, he is a monster because the British made him that way. The question the film partially succeeds in raising is whether this insistence on past wrongs can continue to justify contemporary acts of violent aggression.

If *The Field* works on one level as a dialogue with Irish historical representation, on another, it engages directly with existing cinematic images of Irishness, most particularly those of perhaps the best-known of all Irish films, *The Quiet Man*. Ford's film represents a fantasy of return which reality would deny most of the Irish-American immigrants of the period in which it was made. Since its release, it has come to enjoy iconic status, consistently appearing on lists of all-time favourite films; it is a significant contributor to the local tourist economy of Cong, where it was filmed. Where Sean Thornton (John Wayne) returned with his few dollars, bought the cottage of his childhood and married the red-haired Irish colleen, in *The Field* the Yank is vilified and eventually killed for attempting the same. In Ford's version, Sean Thornton represents rational, American modernity; he will, as Sheridan comments, rescue the girl from the "incest culture" (see interview). However, he can only become accepted in that culture when he undergoes the rites of initiation symbolised by participation in the "donnybrook", or communal brawl. In *The Field*, the red-haired colleen has been banished to the margins of the narrative where she lurks as the jeering, vampish Tinker Girl, more Banshee than Bean an Tí. Irish violence in Ford's vision is wholesome and cathartic, a spectacle open to all participants. It is a communal, masculine activity like pub-brawling and drunken song. Violence, as we have seen in *The Field*, however, leads only to tragedy.

In its characterisation of the community as idle and menacing, *The Field* very specifically deconstructs Ford's idyllic world. In his films, community is posited as an ideal, its rituals closely observed, and its vulnerability only offset by the loyalty it inspires in its defenders. Sheridan's version of this is to emphasise the poverty of spirit that he sees as endemic to rural Ireland. He particularly insists on the inwardness of the locals; even the Widow is jeered ("Ya hoor, you") by a bystander and both she and the priest, outsiders like the Yank, are consistently seen to be refused admission to the

closed circle of the true natives. The role of the tinkers who
provide a leering chorus as they demand their blood money
renders them as the ghosts of the past, malevolent relics of
pre-Christian Ireland, although as the Priest (Sean McGinley)
tells the Yank of the community as a whole, "There's just a
thin veneer of Christianity been painted on these people." In
this respect, his film is much closer to Lean's *Ryan's Daughter*, another work that explores the consequences of an outsider entering a remote Irish community. Lean's film too
ends with the death of the outsider, in addition to the dis-
gracing of the local woman who became his lover. Many critics picked up on the similarities between the two works,
reading John Hurt's Bird O'Donnell as a reprise of the similar role of Michael, the village idiot, played by John Mills in
Ryan's Daughter.

A recurrent trope of *The Quiet Man* is the local population's and Mary-Kate Danaher's (Maureen O'Hara) oneness
with nature. The celebrated opening sequences, where Sean
Thornton gets his first glimpse of Mary-Kate, position her as
something of a Dresden maiden, herding her flock of sheep
through the lush Irish meadows. Sean Thornton courts her
against the violent backdrop of a storm, and the donnybrook
takes place in the outdoors where participants are confined
neither by space or regulations. Certainly, the pivotal scene
in *The Field*, in which the Bull murders the Yank at the foot
of the waterfall at night, recalls this association between the
Irish temperament and natural forces; yet now nature has
become associated with death.

The anachronistic Bull is seen to be at one with his environment, but the rest of the community is associated with
interior spaces or confined to the small village in which the
action takes place. For Bull, the land, and particularly the field,
are what he is still fighting for: "It's my field, it's my child, I
nursed it". The Yank has no empathy with the rural either and
wants to cement over the land and commercialise it.

Other scenes, such as the opening sequences where the Bull and Tadgh haul creels of seaweed off the rocks and up the mountainside and, later, when the Bull sells his turf to the islandmen, recall *Man of Aran* (Robert Flaherty, UK, 1934), another pivotal film in the construction of a cinematic vision of Irishness. Where Flaherty's film is celebrated for its ennobling of the inhabitants of the west of Ireland, Sheridan, as we have seen, is determined to deconstruct this process of romanticisation. Then again, *The Field* has overtones of a literary work that is axiomatic to fictional representations of the west of Ireland, *The Playboy of the Western World*. Tadgh's lie, that it was he who killed the Yank, persuades the tinker girl to make love to him, recalling Christy Mahon's similar ruse in the earlier play.

The Field is certainly a flawed work, yet its aspiration to demolish many of the shibboleths of Irish historical and cinematic representation renders it a fascinating film. Its most striking paradox lies in the fact that, as much as it re-claims the past, it argues that to live in the present we must stop looking backwards or be driven insane. In retrospect, it now appears as one of Sheridan's strongest, least sentimen-tal and most questioning works; if it fails to interrogate the immediate social and political conditions of Ireland of the period, instead referring endlessly backwards to colonisation and the Famine, it also problematises its own terms of refer-ence as it establishes them. Further, it consistently attempts to destabilise existing images of Irishness and to give Irish cinema a truly mythic, tragic but ultimately pathetic hero.

Chapter Three

In the Name of the Father (1993): A Political Cinema?

Sheridan's third film, *In the Name of the Father*, marks a number of distinct breaks with his two previous works. It was made after he and Noel Pearson had parted company and was therefore produced as well as directed by Sheridan under the aegis of his new production company, Hell's Kitchen, which he co-founded with Arthur Lappin. It was Sheridan's first film to be financed by a Hollywood studio (Universal Pictures); and it marked the beginning of a three-film collaboration between him and scriptwriter, later director, Terry George, the second work being *Some Mother's Son*, which was directed by George in 1996, followed by *The Boxer*, directed by Sheridan in 1997. George and Sheridan are jointly credited as scriptwriters on all three films. This trilogy of films based around Northern Irish themes marks a period of self-conscious political intervention, which is reflected in this new creative partnership.

Terry George is a former prisoner who was interned as a teenager and later served three years of a six-year sentence on a firearms charge. He was incarcerated in Long Kesh (the Maze) in the period prior to the establishment of the notorious H-Blocks and the introduction of the policy of criminalisation, which was eventually to lead to the hunger strikes. His time, therefore, was spent in "the Cages", where political prisoners essentially ran their own regime, enjoying free association and attending classes in Irish and political education. Following his release, George read history and politics at Queen's University, where he became involved in student protests sparked off by the hunger strikes and did not complete his degree. Following the assassination of his political mentor, Miriam Daly, a member of the IRSP, and the discovery that his name was on a loyalist deathlist, George and his wife and young child left Belfast for New York where, as an illegal immigrant, he worked in the inevitable occupations of taxi driver, bartender and on building sites. There he wrote *The Tunnel*, a stage play based on an attempted escape from the Cages, which Jim Sheridan directed at the New York Arts Center.

To appreciate the impact this trilogy of films, particularly *In the Name of the Father*, had on public opinion, it is important to understand how difficult it was to discuss any political issues in the media that touched on the Troubles, particularly from within a popular medium such as film. Whilst the Troubles have been widely documented in moving images on news programmes and television generally, they have also suffered from massive censorship and, specifically, from self-censorship. From the early days of the Civil Rights marches, news cameras accompanied and observed participants, and their images were broadcast across TV channels world-wide. Paul Bew and Gordon Gillespie have written of the Derry Civil Rights march of 1968 that:

> The events in Derry on 5 October 1968 opened up the modern Ulster crisis. The television coverage — especially the work of RTÉ cameraman Gay O'Brien — changed the course of Northern Ireland history. The media gave widespread coverage to the unre-

> strained batoning by the RUC of demonstrators, in-
> cluding MPs, without "justification or excuse" (ac-
> cording to the Cameron Commission). The percep-
> tion rapidly developed that something was rotten in
> the state of Northern Ireland. (Bew and Gillespie,
> 1993: 4)

Whilst newsreel footage continued to be widely circulated, the points of view of the paramilitaries long went unheard and their representatives unseen. Section 31 of the Irish Broadcasting Act of 1960 was updated in 1976 to prevent the appearance of interviews or reports of interviews with spokespersons from the spectrum of paramilitary groups and their political representatives (the IRA, Sinn Féin, the UDA, the INLA and so on) and was only repealed in 1994. As early as 1972, the government had made its position clear by dismissing the entire RTÉ Authority for broadcasting an interview with IRA Chief of Staff, Seán Mac Stiofáin. Subsequently, in 1988, journalist Jenny McGeever was dismissed for including an interview with Sinn Féin member, Martin McGuinness, as part of a report on the aftermath of the Gibraltar killings (where three unarmed IRA suspects were shot dead by the SAS). A further tool of Irish government censorship has been the Official Secrets Act of 1963.

In the UK, although the Prevention of Terrorism Act (1974) did deter many journalists from interviewing suspected terrorists, censorship was less a matter of legislation than tacit consent between various government bodies and the media. As the authors of *Televising "Terrorism"* conclude:

> The British way of censorship relies upon a mediated
> intervention which sustains the legitimacy and the
> credibility both of the state and of the broadcasting
> institutions. Naturally, this has a price for the state,
> which has managed to secure only indirect and par-
> tial control of broadcasting's output. But it has nev-

> ertheless significantly defined the terms of reference
> under which the broadcasters operate, and in this
> respect the project of excluding its republican ene-
> mies from the air as much as possible has in practice
> been very successful. (Schlesinger, Murdock, Elliott,
> 1983: 129)

These official pronouncements from above combined with
stringent self-censorship from within meant that, until recently, paramilitaries have at best been represented by an
actor's voice over a scrambled image. Documentaries on
issues related to the Troubles have consistently been subjected to intense scrutiny from the highest echelons of the
British government, with some, such as *Edge of the Union*
(which carried an interview with Martin McGuinness) and
Death on the Rock (about the Gibraltar shootings), made in
1985 by BBC Television and 1988 by Thames Television respectively, becoming *causes célèbres* in the battle between
programme makers and the state. Fictional representations,
too, have had to tread warily around constrictions and many
television plays in particular have run into difficulties when it
came to broadcasting. The intrusion of Troubles-related issues and footage has even resulted in censorship being applied to mainstream programmes including *Top of the Pops*
and *Eastenders* (Curtis and Jempson, 1993). Even without
these constrictions, filmmakers have been reluctant to engage with the minefield of Northern Irish politics and the
belief that the Troubles make for poor box-office has been
generally accepted.

Suspicions about the nature of images of the Troubles
have thus accompanied their ubiquity. As Brian McAvera
wrote in his introduction to the *Directions Out* exhibition of
1988:

> In Northern Ireland there is no shortage of photo-
> graphic images which depict the Troubles. They con-

front us daily in our newspapers and magazines, sidle obsessively into our livingrooms by way of television, and, like recalcitrant children who refuse to go away, there they are when we turn to the English or European media. Living in the North (or I imagine in any location which had become a focus for the media) repeatedly reinforces an awareness of how photographic images simplify, distort and devalue. . . . What is worse is the urge-to-believe — seeing is believing — enshrined within the naturalistic surface of the image. . . . When added to this is the power of the word, whether in caption form or commentary, the result is a powerful tool — and ideological weapon — be it subtle or overt. (McAvera, 1988: unpaginated)

In this climate, the release of two feature films in succession that portrayed real events and characters in a manner that reflected not just a little negatively on the British establishment was, as Sheridan recollects, a shock to the IRA as much as to their enemies:

The thing about that was that everyone lived with the fact that the IRA couldn't be on television. So they were used to not being allowed to say anything and suddenly they see this film and it's like from outer space. It's kind of saying what they want to say and they are afraid to say, although they wouldn't exactly say it the way I did it. The IRA man would have been nicer in the film but I think it was a shock as much to them as it was to the British system. (see interview)

In the Name of the Father is loosely based on Gerry Conlon's book, Proved Innocent, and covers the notorious miscarriage of justice that ensued in the wake of the bombing of two pubs in Guildford in October of 1974. As part of a campaign of attacking what it considered to be legitimate targets in

England, the IRA had planted the bombs in pubs allegedly used by off-duty soldiers. They exploded without warning, killing five people and injuring 54. In the following month, 19 people were killed on the spot and 182 injured in bombs placed in Birmingham pubs, and it was in the wake of the latter bombing that the British government introduced the Prevention of Terrorism Act, allowing suspected terrorists to be held without charge for seven days and also to be expelled from Britain. Both bombings outraged public opinion and the British police came under pressure to bring the perpetrators to justice.

They swiftly arrested three groups of people who were to become known as the Guildford Four, the Maguire Seven and the Birmingham Six. The Guildford Four were sentenced to life imprisonment in October 1975; the Maguire Seven, a family accused of making bombs on behalf of the Guildford Four, were jailed in 1976 on foot of information allegedly supplied by Gerry Conlon whilst under interrogation by the police; and the Birmingham Six were imprisoned in July 1975, despite admissions from the prosecution that they had been seriously assaulted whilst in custody. All three cases were taken up by pressure groups within Ireland and the United Kingdom who claimed that the so-called perpetrators of these bombings and their alleged accomplices had been forced to sign confessions and brutalised whilst in police custody.

A number of fictionalised accounts and television documentaries were made at the time to highlight these miscarriages of justice, including *Dear Sarah* (RTÉ, 1990) and *Who Bombed Birmingham?* (Granada TV, 1990). Indeed, pressure from the British media in general was one of the factors that led to the re-opening of the various cases. The Guildford Four were eventually cleared of their charges and released in October 1989, although one of them, Paul Hill, was held for a longer period pending the resolution of another case in which he was implicated. The Court of Appeal pronounced that the 1975 convictions were based on fabricated testimonies and that scientific evidence that might have cleared the accused had been withheld by the Director of Public Prosecutions of the time. This in turn cast doubt on the convictions of the Maguire Seven, who had to wait until 1991 to be finally cleared by the Court of Appeal. Gerry Conlon's father, Guiseppe Conlon, who had been imprisoned as part of the swoop on the Maguire Seven, had meanwhile died in prison.

The case against the Maguire Seven was regarded with particular bitterness, given that the report into the miscarriages of justice headed by Sir John May failed to establish beyond doubt that the Maguires were innocent. They had been convicted of running a bomb factory in their home on the basis of evidence that suggested that traces of nitroglycerine had been found on a used hand-towel; whilst the scientific procedure employed to make this case was widely discredited long before their release, the failure of the May report to endorse these findings did little to re-establish confidence in the British justice system.

The Birmingham Six were freed in March of 1991 after it was proved that the West Midlands Police had fabricated evidence in order to indict them. The reluctance of the British establishment to take full responsibility for their handling of the three cases was highlighted not only by the inadequate response to the freeing of the Maguire Seven but also by their failure to bring to justice the police officers responsible for fabricating evidence and brutalising the victims whilst they were in custody. In 1993, the former detectives in charge of the Guildford Four Case were cleared of the charge of conspiracy to pervert the course of justice; and in the same year, the three former policemen who faced similar charges in relation to the Birmingham Six case had their trial terminated by the judge who felt that the surrounding media coverage would not allow for a fair hearing. Thus, although the events portrayed in *In the Name of the Father* were officially over by the time of the film's making, it could be argued that full closure had not been reached, given the climate of denial circulating within the higher echelons of British policy-making.

In the Name of the Father focuses on one strand of these events, namely Gerry Conlon's involvement with them, and in particular, the playing out of the relationship between Gerry and his father, Guiseppe, whilst they shared a prison cell. The film opens with the explosion in one of the Guild-ford pubs and then moves back in time and place to Gerry's youth in Belfast. In an extended sequence, we see him run-ning away from British soldiers who have mistaken him for a sniper instead of the petty thief that he was (in this instance, he had been robbing lead from rooftops). Hearing that the IRA plan to kneecap him, Gerry skips to England, meeting up with Paul Hill, a friend from school, on the way. Initially, they live in a squat in London but after they are thrown out, they take to sleeping rough in a park. There they meet the Irish tramp Charlie Burke, who presciently warns them of the dangers of staying too long in London: "There's nothing for me there [Ireland] now." Shortly afterwards, and following Gerry's theft of money from a prostitute, they return to Belfast, revelling in their wealth and their new-found taste for hippie-style clothing — Gerry's ludicrous but chic Afghan coat. It is there that they are arrested, deported and forced to confess to the bombings. The two young men and two other members of their squat are imprisoned on the basis of these testimonies. The emotional core of the film follows as Gerry and Guiseppe are forced to share a cell and Gerry gradually moves from resentment of his father's passivity to respect for it. Following his father's death, Gerry co-operates with the lawyer Gareth Peirce (Emma Thompson) who, following a courtroom drama, effects the release of the four prisoners.

In a detailed and engaging analysis of the film, Martin McLoone has demonstrated that, such was its controversial reception (discussed below), its narrative and aesthetics were ignored (McLoone, 1994: 45). McLoone recognises the film's dilemma, that, in order to satisfy the requirements of Hollywood, genre-based filmmaking, it had to compromise its politics. Thus, the father–son relationship dominates the work to the neglect of its political-historical background. In a commercial environment that privileges genre and actor, the film "taps into the 'men-without-women' prison drama genre, where the quest for justice becomes a journey of self-discovery — a kind of *Cool Hand Luke* [Stuart Rosenberg, US, 1967] for the Nineties" (ibid.).

Further, *In the Name of the Father* offers its viewers another opportunity to relish the thespian skills of Daniel Day-Lewis as well as an emotional performance by Pete Postlethwaite as Guiseppe, and musician Don Baker's turn as the steely-eyed IRA prisoner. Sheridan has acknowledged this aspect of the film, drawing attention to the practicalities of financing a political fable about the British dimension of the Northern Irish Troubles; asked in interview whether it was difficult to get backing for this story, he replied:

> Yes, until I had Daniel it was difficult, but Daniel made it a lot easier. Fundamentally I don't think it meant much to the Americans. They were interested enough in the father–son side of it. Nobody is really interested in an injustice story. It is a difficult story to tell. But the father–son story is not so difficult. (Linehan, 1993/94: 12)

Recognising the effectiveness of these central performances and the inclusion of an element of political discourse (the IRA prisoner is distinguished from other inmates on the grounds that he is motivated by politics rather than crime), McLoone concludes that, "Sheridan is undoubtedly a director who has politics . . . but he is not a political filmmaker and *In the Name of the Father* is not a consciously political film" (McLoone, 1994: 46).

McLoone's critique of Sheridan's filmmaking needs to be set against a wider sense of disappointment prevalent in film studies that cinema, with a few exceptions, has abandoned that commitment to radical left-wing politics that character-ised a certain element in filmmaking in the 1960s and 1970s. It was this movement that informed the avant-garde cinema of the first wave of indigenous Irish filmmakers in the 1970s and early 1980s, resulting in politically engaged works such as Bob Quinn's *Caoineadh Airt Uí Laoire* (Ireland, 1975) and Pat Murphy's *Maeve* (UK, 1981).

Although McLoone concludes his article with a call to a return to political filmmaking, suggesting that only an indige-nously funded industry can produce these works, in reality, it has to be acknowledged that such a turn of events is un-likely. This kind of filmmaking requires either private or gov-ernment funding and access to a sympathetic audience. It is questionable whether either now exists. The sort of Brechtian cinema that is associated with this movement de-limits its own audience and, arguably, simply preaches to the converted. A filmmaker who wishes to engage a wider group of viewers must, of necessity, make concessions in terms of artistic practices. Even in the 1970s, these issues were clear, with filmmakers tending to fall into one of two camps.On the one hand, there existed the intellectually challenging, artistically deconstructive cinema of Godard in France, and, on the other, the more mainstream practice of Costa-Gavras which produced works such as *Z* (France/Algeria, 1968) and the later *Missing* (US, 1981). Somewhere in be-tween, and the template for many later filmmakers, was Gillo Pontecorvo's *The Battle of Algiers* (Algeria/Italy, 1965) with its attempt to humanise the FLN and the French equally, its notion of a collective hero and its endorsement of violent insurrection. Of these filmmakers, Costa-Gavras makes the greatest concessions to a mainstream audience, offering sympathetic central characters, an identifiable enemy and high levels of narrative suspense. He called for a new kind of cinema which would try "to explain the historical situation and all the connections which lead to that kind of history", whilst justifying his own approach to filmmaking on the grounds that "you don't catch flies with vinegar" (Georgakas and Rubenstein, 1983: 69, 72). His two films mentioned above carry a very clear humanist message as well as detailing the specifics of, respectively, the 1965 Lambrakis Affair and the Chilean coup of 1973. However, whilst they met with critical approval in many quarters, they were equally critiqued for "dressing up" their political message. Thus, Julian Petley writes of Gavras's cinema:

> The problem is that by substituting narrative suspense for political analysis, by stressing action at the expense of historical context and background, and by playing out complex ideological conflicts within a simplistic good-versus-evil moral framework, his films seriously risk becoming less a means of political enlightenment than thrillers with superficially political plots. (Petley, 1981: 1617)

The populist basis of Hollywood filmmaking consistently expresses itself through the theme of the individual against the system. Human agency in Hollywood films is also commonly assumed to be a consequence of personal, psychological traits rather than social or historical conditioning, or at least in terms of the hero (the villain may be villainous simply as a result of ethnicity, gender or class). Clearly, American financing, combined with the need to appeal to the lucrative Hollywood market, has tended to impose this format on films such as *In the Name of the Father*.

But the film also reached an audience that an equivalent *avant-garde* work could never have dreamed of reaching. In Ireland, it was a national event, taking €3.05 million in the cinemas which made it the second-highest-grossing Irish film to date after *Michael Collins* (Neil Jordan, US, 1996) (Barton, 2001: 31). In the US, the film took $24 million on its theatrical release on a budget of $13 million, a modest sum by Hollywood standards, but nearly twice as much as *My Left Foot* (Dean, 1994: 14). It received seven Academy Award nominations: three for Jim Sheridan (producer, director, and, with Terry George, co-scriptwriter); one each for Daniel Day-Lewis (Best Actor), Pete Postlethwaite (Best Supporting Actor), Emma Thompson (Best Supporting Actress) and Gerry Hambling (Best Film Editing) in the same year that Steven Spielberg's *Schindler's List* (US, 1993), another popularised version of history, ultimately swept the board.

In the United Kingdom, the box-office figures were lower and the combined total for the UK and Ireland was around stg£4.5 million (Screen International, 1994: 50). The popular success of *In the Name of the Father* in Ireland (these figures cover both North and South of the border) suggests that, as a text, it resonated significantly with audiences in Ireland and with its other designated target market, the US.

Certainly, the film's appeal can be partially attributed to its adherence to mainstream filmmaking practices and its recourse, as in *My Left Foot*, to a high emotional register. It is technically competent and boasts exceptional performances. Yet it seems unwise to write off its politics; they may indeed lurk behind a set of representational codes that distance critical judgement. Indeed, the hostility with which the film was greeted by some quarters within the UK and others in the US needs to be read against certain positions the film was taking. In particular, its suggestion that the British State was capable of engaging in actions that were as reprehensible as those generally associated with paramilitary activity — physi-

cal torture, mental abuse and the taking of innocent lives —
locates the film within a very small niche of critics of an institution that has, during the course of the Troubles, successfully deflected attention from its less salubrious policies.

The focus of In the Name of the Father is certainly the
father–son relationship. Through the course of the film,
Gerry moves from a rejection of all patriarchal control (in
his role of petty thief) to a brief capitulation to the authority
of the British police (when he is cradled by the police officer,
Dixon (Corin Redgrave) under interrogation), to his admiration for the IRA leader Joe McAndrew and subsequent dis-
enchantment when McAndrew sets alight the sympathetic
prison officer, to eventual reconciliation with his own father
whose place he takes (in campaigning for their release) after
Guiseppe's death.

The rejection of the violent father for the pacifist is also
an ideological trajectory, the point where Gerry abandons
his (misplaced, the film suggests) admiration of IRA tactics.
Gerry's other symbolic father, police officer Dixon, is an
unremittingly evil character. Even his name could hardly be
fortuitous and the entire encounter between him and Gerry
deliberately subverts the general trend of British television
representations of the police as benevolent figures; as Conlon muses in Proved Innocent, "this I thought, was England,
home of Dixon of Dock Green and Z Cars . . . I still had this
belief in English justice and decency. Wasn't it on the TV all
through my childhood?" (Conlon, 1990: 108). The film's rejection of Dixon as a father figure for Conlon, which he
might well have become in a standard police drama, is not
just an oedipal one but a political statement: a denial of the
legitimacy of British authority and, in a secondary manner, of
its re-enforcement through the official media.

The prison offers Gerry a surrogate family within which
to make his oedipal passage. The Jamaicans become his
brothers (and fellow outsiders) and, in the scene following

Guiseppe's death, where we see hundreds of flaming paper tributes floating down from the prison windows in the darkness, the communality of prison life is stressed. To underline the point, the prisoners are watching *The Godfather* (Francis Ford Coppola, US, 1974), a film that links criminality with male bonding. McLoone has suggested that the reference to *The Godfather* functions to demarcate McAndrew from the other prisoners, in so far as it prompts the viewer to distinguish, as the Corleones do, between politically motivated anti-state activities and those undertaken for mere criminal gain (McLoone, 1994: 46). Part of the power of Coppola's gangster trilogy is to reflect on the system of honour that binds the criminal family — at first admirable, it soon is revealed to be regressive and morally imprisoning. This is something that Gerry must also understand; naturally drawn to the prison group, he will, in the end, replace the bad family with the good, his own.

Whilst the father–son relationship is the key to the film's dramatic success, we also have to ask to what extent it carries historical and symbolic resonances similar to those discussed in the previous two chapters. In answer to this, Sheridan has said that:

> I like the title *In the Name of the Father* because it implies "and of the son" . . . When I first read the script, I got fascinated by the father–son side of it.

> The idea behind the film is that the father figure becomes a kind of decimated symbol when you have a crushed culture. Once you destroy the father figure, the figure of authority, then you haven't got a society. It's about trying to restore a man who believes in non-violence and peace and will suffer rather than inflict suffering . . .

> Here's a father and a son, an aunt, an uncle and two nephews — a whole family in prison and yet we in-

sist on calling them the Guildford Four and the Maguire Seven. How can you split a family into component parts? Once you do that, you start destroying society. (Dwyer, 1993: 1)

We can read this comment in several ways. As in Sheridan's other films, the family becomes metonymic for the nation. The "crushed culture", if it is that of Northern Irish republican society, is thus indicted as a classic victim of colonial disempowerment. If, in the previous chapter, we saw how Sheridan signalled that post-independence Ireland had failed to free itself of the structures of its colonial past, here he seems to suggest that Northern Ireland has still to achieve even post-colonial status.

Margot Gayle Backus, in her essay on *In the Name of the Father*, considers that Guiseppe represents the traditional figure of the prison martyr, although she omits to highlight the religious/historical resonances this role carries with it (Backus, 1999: 58). The religious overtones in the altered title echo throughout the film in the themes of sacrifice and redemption: "When I got Holy Communion, I thought I was eating you alive," Gerry remarks to his father. Implicit in his rejection of Guiseppe is his rejection of the role of Catholic martyr. As we shall see, a similar rejection occurs in *Some Mother's Son* when Kathleen refuses to adopt the position of mother/martyr.

In a further reconfiguration of the religious narrative, Gerry is redeemed through his father's sacrifice. Guiseppe is the all-forgiving father of the more benign versions of Christianity whose moral authority Gerry must accede to in order to reach redemption. In common with the figure of Mrs Brown in *My Left Foot*, the character of Guiseppe is endowed with multiple meanings. He is not just the "divine" father of Christianity but the conventional dispossessed male of post-colonial representational practices. Where the Bull McCabe expressed his disenfranchised status as post-colonial subject through destructive rage, Guiseppe recognises that he is an unfree citizen who is indentured to a colonial system. This system has consigned Guiseppe to a slow death (doubly so, in fact, since his relegation to the kind of low-paid work which caused his lung disease was consequent upon his religious status in Northern Ireland). Sheridan has articulated this aspect of the film's symbolic structure thus:

> Societies and religions are structured around father images. England became a kind of father figure whom the Irish have been trying to confront for a long time. I believe that England's centuries of domination over Ireland have undermined the Irish father's authority. The children of weak or compromised fathers are often forced to escape — if they can — or face becoming the very thing they despise. (McAlpine, 1993: 11)

Gerry's need to leave Northern Ireland is an escape from a society of emasculated fathers, but he ends up in the arms of the bad paternal state. Ironically, he must recognise the potential efficacy of British justice by putting his trust in the lawyer Gareth Peirce. As we shall see, this device of collapsing several of the real-life individuals who secured the release of the Guildford Four into that of Peirce, was one of the levers which the film's critics used to discredit it. However, in symbolic terms, it is essential that the lawyer be female and thus distinct from the bad father/British patriarchal state. Her lawless methods of information gathering — snooping in the files and uncovering the crucial hidden evidence — reinforce the suggestion that the legitimating structures of the British state may only be breached by finding an alternative way through them.

There is, however, a weakness in *In the Name of the Father*'s indictment of the British establishment, a weakness that re-emerges in *Some Mother's Son* and brings us back to McLoone's contention that Sheridan is not a political film-maker. The problem is that the intense father–son relationship establishes the central confrontation as being between Gerry and Guiseppe rather than between the Guildford Four, the Maguire Seven and the State. This need not have been; the film could have remained within generic territory simply by positioning itself as a conspiracy thriller, a format with honourable antecedents in works that critique the US political establishment — *The Conversation* (Francis Coppola, US, 1974), *The Parallax View* (Alan J. Pakula, US, 1974) — and even those made from within British cinema such as *Defence of the Realm* (David Drury, UK, 1985). Sheridan may have been forced into this construction by funding requirements, but the fact that his work in general is structured around oedipal conflicts worked out within the symbolic family suggests that his inclinations naturally lay in this direction.

In *Some Mother's Son*, the same displacement of the political conflict takes place. The latter film, co-scripted and produced, as we have noted, by Sheridan, and directed by Terry George, is a fictionalised account of the 1981 hunger strikes. It was in fact written prior to *In the Name of the Father*, though produced afterwards. The film was the first in a cycle of films to filter recent Northern Irish history through the consciousness of a female character (in this case, two female characters) and, according to Terry George, drew on his experiences of growing up in Northern Ireland:

> The mother–son relationship in the film is definitely influenced by what I thought my mother had to endure and what all the mothers had to endure in both communities. Mothers are physically asked to clean up after their children and then when they grow up they have to somehow morally clean up after them, support their actions, offer support in prison. (Martin, 1997: 25)

He was also conscious that his film would be seen as a companion piece to *In the Name of the Father*; its title alone invites the comparison:

> The difference between the two is that you have a
> very clear black and white injustice in *In the Name of
> the Father*. This is a much greyer film in that nobody
> is right and everybody is right. That's something I
> was trying to show — everyone is right in Northern
> Ireland from their own position, we're all imbued
> with the righteousness of our own stance. (ibid)

Some Mother's Son concerns the fate of two IRA volunteers, Gerard Quigley (Aidan Gillen) and Frank Higgins (David O'Hara) who are tried and convicted for the murder of a British soldier whilst resisting arrest. The trial brings together their mothers: one, Kathleen Quigley (Helen Mirren) is a widowed, middle-class schoolteacher who had no idea that her son was involved with the IRA. The other, Annie Higgins (Fionnuala Flanagan) comes from a staunch IRA family and has already lost one son in the Troubles. Their sons, in the tradition of IRA volunteers, refuse to acknowledge the jurisdiction of the court and are sent to Long Kesh prison; shortly afterwards, the "dirty protest" is initiated. This is represented within the film as being the outcome of British intransigence; those prisoners who refuse to wear prison clothing on the grounds that they are prisoners of war, not criminals, are brought to the brink when the authorities respond by refusing to slop them out. Inculcated in the policies of Thatcherism — "isolation, criminalisation, demoralisation" — the officials at the Northern Ireland Office refuse to back down and the hunger strikes are initiated.

Eventually, when their own sons join the strike, both mothers must face the decision as to whether or not to allow them to die or whether to sign the permission document that will enable the prison authorities to feed them.

Kathleen signs, Annie does not. *Some Mother's Son* is faithful to much of the detail of this period. Thus, when Gerard meets Bobby Sands (John Lynch), he exclaims, "You look like Jesus Christ"; by the end of the film, Gerard too looks like Bobby Sands/Jesus Christ. To underline this theme, the film has the British diplomat, Harrington (Tim Woodward), demand of the civil servant, Farnsworth (Tom Hollander), after Sands's death, "Do you know anything about the role of Irish martyrs in history — 1916, Pearse, Connolly? Well, you've created another one." In allowing Gerard's mother to save, and thus control, her son's life, the film not only is accurate to history (the strike collapsed as a succession of families refused to let their sons die), but also subverts the idealised figure of the sorrowing Irish widow/mother, so cloyingly eulogised in the verse of Patrick Pearse.

By placing the two mothers at the centre of the narrative, the film is able to establish a three-way dynamic of power. On one side, there is the state/terrorist opposition; on the other lies the IRA who exercise some, although not complete, control over their sons' lives; and, finally, on the outer limits, there exists the Catholic Church whose traditional authority is increasingly challenged by the IRA and individual members of the community. The state is represented through the iconic figure of Margaret Thatcher who, in a pre-credit piece of news footage, delivers her election victory speech of 1979: "I will strive unceasingly to fulfil the trust and confidence that the British people have put in me", she intones, as the crowd cheers (and in the background a few boos are heard) and the cameras flash. From this frenetic metropolitan setting, the film cuts to an idealised image of a small trawler entering harbour in the late afternoon sun. In long shot, the camera reveals the emptiness of the sea and landscape, infiltrated only by the continuing voice of Mrs Thatcher, as she recites the prayer of St Francis of Assisi. As her words come to an end, the soundtrack segues into a

traditional Irish tune composed by Sheridan's long-time musical collaborator, and the man most associated with the
Riverdance phenomenon, Bill Whelan. Beaten out to the
sound of the bodhrán, or traditional Irish drum, and accompanied by the pipes, this musical motif recurs at strategic
moments throughout the film, most controversially in the
scene where the class of schoolgirls in an Irish dancing class
is intercut in slow motion with Gerard and Frank's attack on
the border post.

For one writer, these scenes were redolent of a giant
sell-out of Irish culture to Hollywood, an endorsement of
violence through its association with children and entertainment, and an elision of its real consequences (White,
1996: 14). The soundtrack certainly is reliant on a sense of
an organic tribal energy that is played out against a succession of images: the primitive/rural, violent action, and communal resistance (the riot that breaks out when Sands dies).

In the Name of the Father, by contrast, locates itself
within an international set of references by drawing on existing popular musical accompaniment, alongside the original
soundtrack by Gavin Friday, Bono et al. The Belfast riot
takes place to the background of Hendrix whilst Gerry's
return home in hippie gear is signalled by the playing of the
ironic Scarlet Pimpernel track, "Dedicated Follower of Fash-
ion" (The Kinks). *Some Mother's Son* establishes a dichotomy
between the rural/native — the seascape, the settings of
both women's homes — and an intrusive state. The meeting
room at the Northern Ireland Office recalls Hollywood representations of CIA headquarters, with its massive map of
the province taking up one wall, its rows of computer ter-
minals, desks and telephones and an overall sense of a
gleaming, technological modernity. The State functionaries
are dressed in tight business suits, emphasising that, for
them, this is a job, not a conviction. They are further associated with the technology of surveillance, walkie-talkies and

infra-red lights, as they stake out the Flanagans' traditional small Irish farmhouse. The violation of the rural by the aggressor state is further suggested in a number of establishing scenes when the British army sets up permanent roadblocks on border crossings. In one, Annie, who with her stocky body and utilitarian clothing is depicted as the traditional Irish countrywoman, is seen herding her cattle down a country lane when a massive concrete block is placed in her path by a regiment of British soldiers.

In common with *In the Name of the Father*, the state is again personified as male. The very English Farnsworth is a particularly fascistic presence within the film. Rigidly devoted to ensuring that his government remain in control of the situation, he has no idea of the issues of humanity at stake, nor does he share the sense of pragmatism expressed by the diplomat, Harrington. Within this configuration, the British army is not the instigator of repression but its tool of implementation. Individually, the soldiers are politically uncommitted, as one of the film's few comic set-pieces suggests. Kathleen takes Annie to the beach for a driving lesson and they bog the car. To the deeply republican Annie's chagrin, their rescuers arrive in the form of a group of soldiers out exercising, who cheerfully lift them out.

The prisoners, on the other hand, are portrayed as passive and almost childlike. They react to Bobby Sands's morning exercise routine, shouted between the cells, with the lack of enthusiasm of any other teenager or youth. And, as their hair grows longer, so their vanishing faces and their increasing physical similarities reflect the sublimation of their personalities to the greater good of the cause. It is their bodies that are at stake here, not what they represent as individuals.

It is control over these bodies that forms the dramatic tension of the film's conclusion. Both the British authorities and the families have the power to end the strike, and, although the standoff includes the IRA and the Church, the film suggests that neither of the latter two agencies has any real control. This structuring device posits nature (maternal love) against artifice (the repressive State), an enormous simplification of the central political issues. The final "will she, won't she?" dilemma, as Kathleen realises all negotiation has failed, removes the State from the frame entirely, leaving Gerard's fate a matter of individual conscience. Whereas the film has taken some pains to document Kathleen's growing politicisation and commensurate loss of faith in democratic institutions, ultimately, she must abandon politics for humanism. Annie, on the other hand, is trapped in an atavistic republican mode of thinking that leaves her, in her own words, with no alternatives: "It's not my choice to make. Jesus Christ, do you think if it was my choice, I'd let him die?"

Some Mother's Son, more than *In the Name of the Father*, is hampered by its fact/fiction relationship. The use of newsreel footage and the device of keeping the viewer abreast of events by introducing snippets of radio news dialogue on the soundtrack, anchor it within a documentary or docudrama tradition. Yet, with the exception of Bobby Sands, Danny Morrison and Frank Maguire, the characters portrayed are fictional. This is particularly true of Kathleen Quigley, given that the hunger strikers all came from working-class backgrounds. Its interpretation of the politics of the hunger strikes — that the IRA leaders on the outside manipulated the strikers — annoyed republicans and was almost certainly inaccurate. The campaign on the streets is widely accepted to have taken second place to the hunger strikers who in turn had become intensely politicised through their encounter with the British and prison authorities (Feldman, 1991: 147–8).

A further simplification has the "dirty protest", when the prisoners started to smear excrement over the cell walls, occur when British government officials up the ante on the blanket protest by announcing that the prisoner officers will no longer slop out the prisoners. In fact, the dirty protest was initiated by the prisoners in response to severe harassment (internal body searching and general tactics of humiliation) organised around their usage of the bathroom and washing facilities (ibid., 147–217). A more general critique of the film is that it fails to indicate the massive importance of the hunger strikes within the history of the Troubles, and in particular, the iconic significance of Bobby Sands.

Although *In the Name of the Father* and *Some Mother's Son* sacrifice political insights to humanist dilemmas, their inclusion of some critique of the oppressive state marks them out as singular. As a number of writers have discussed, the IRA campaign in Northern Ireland has consistently been depicted on film as atavistic and tribal (Hill, 1987; McLoone, 2000). Such representations are not restricted to cinema but reflect a wider social and historical failure to recognise that republican violence in particular could have its roots in contemporary economic or political conditions. Filmmakers have simply mirrored a commonly held set of opinions when they have suggested that it is in the nature of the Irish to enjoy a fight. On the one hand, they have focused on the metaphysics of violence (in, say, the work of Neil Jordan: *Angel* (Ireland, 1982) and *The Crying Game* (UK, 1992)); while, on the other, they have examined its internecine nature (*Cal* (Pat O'Connor, UK, 1984), *Nothing Personal* (Thaddeus O'Sullivan, Ireland, 1995)).

This has left the British authorities conveniently out of the picture, thus disarming in advance any suggestion that their agents might be as assiduously engaged in acts of violence as are the terrorists they are committed to oppose. Only the recent *Bloody Sunday* (Paul Greengrass, UK/Ireland. 2002; co-produced by Hell's Kitchen) and *Sunday* (Jimmy McGovern, Channel 4, 2002) make this point with some force, with their critique of the paratroopers' actions in

Derry in January 1972. *Sunday* also suggests that the failure
of the Widgery inquiry to recognise the paratroopers' guilt
was instrumental in persuading large numbers of the Derry
citizenry to enlist with the IRA.

It is common knowledge amongst those involved that
the agents of the British government, in particular the army
paratrooper regiments and those responsible for interrogat-
ing prisoners, have been brutal in their response to paramilitary insurgency. These techniques are merely suggested in *In
the Name of the Father* and may be considered synecdochic
for a range of similar practices commonly applied within
Northern Ireland. Similarly, the incursion of the political into
the domestic rehearsed in Kathleen Quigley's encounter
with the military and the State is a reminder of the much
more brutal intrusions regularly performed in house-to-
house searches in the North.

The reluctance of films like *In the Name of the Father* and
Some Mother's Son to go for the jugular in this respect re-
flects a liberal-humanist desire to achieve ideological balance.
Both are keen to distance themselves from the practice of
IRA terrorism; Don Baker's IRA man, Joe McAndrew, is a
classic psychopath, in the mould of, say, Sean Lenihan (James
Cagney) in *Shake Hands with the Devil* (Michael Anderson,
UK, 1959) or the later Sean Miller (Sean Bean) in *Patriot
Games* (Phillip Noyce, US, 1992); while the common suffering of the bereaved on either side of the political divide is
voiced by Kathleen Quigley when she confronts Gerard
about the death of the British soldier in the raid on the Higgins's home, saying that he "was somebody's son, like you're
mine". The somewhat schematic inclusion of the murder of
two prison officers, one in front of his family, whose ghosts
haunt Kathleen when she must make up her mind whether
or not to remove Gerard from the hunger strike, brings the
point home. The drawback to pursuing balance is that you
may end up pleasing no-one. As one critic wrote:

> . . . the problem, as ever, in dealing with Northern
> Ireland is that by telling one story, you invite castiga-
> tion for not telling all the others. In a place of dia-
> metrically opposed traditions, both sides will trawl
> through any work of art looking for crumbs of self-
> justification as well as sins of omission: the demands
> of political one-upmanship are such that everyone
> wants to be right, and if a film doesn't endorse your
> particular opinion, then you have to make a point of
> dismissing it. Simply responding to it "as a film" isn't
> in it, when cultural trophy-taking is an integral ele-
> ment of one's ideological self-definition. (Johnston,
> 1996, 51)

The thrust of both films is to suggest that constitutional resistance is more satisfactory than terrorism, yet neither can
subscribe fully to that dictum. What Gerry Conlon discovers
from his father's death and his encounter with McAndrew is
that action taken from within the judicial system is more
effective and humane than lawless violence. Thus, he pursues
his case through the courts with the aid of Gareth Peirce
and achieves victory along the kind of lines his father would
have approved of. There are of course flaws in this type of
argument in that it could be said that the Guildford Four
were "lucky" to have their case resolved by the judiciary and
that other similar victims have been less fortunate. As the
film suggests in its closing titles, those who perpetrated this
injustice have not been punished and, thus, the larger question, of the ability of the British Establishment to deal fairly
with the Irish, remains hinted at but not fully explored.

In Some Mother's Son, the message is even more opaque.
Kathleen moves from a belief in the system, symbolised by
her appointment of a barrister to defend Gerard (who refuses to be represented), through her support for Bobby
Sands's electoral campaign, to participation in various dem-
onstrations organised to highlight the hunger strikes. To the

end, she remains hopeful that negotiation will prevail, taking her case, with Annie Higgins, to Westminster and acting as liaison between the British diplomat and the IRA. All these constitutional avenues, however, fail her, as does the Catholic Church (an institution for which the film has little sympathy). Where will she go after this? The scene in which she removes the stone from her younger son's hand in the riot indicates that it will not be down the path of violence, yet, her alternatives are limited. In many ways, we might conclude that Kathleen Quigley's position reflects that of the SDLP with their republican aspirations and their commitment to non-violent intervention. Annie Higgins, on the other hand, is consigned to the recidivist world of traditional republican politics, where she must remain, it is suggested, less from ideological reasons than because that is the role history has allotted her.

Sheridan has suggested that his liberal-humanist middle-ground escaped the attentions of the British media when they launched their attack on *In the Name of the Father* and that he had indeed made the British establishment seem more "humane" than it actually was (see interview). His hope that, "verbal opposition disarms the violence and therefore the more you talk about it in pictures, the more control you have over the uncontrollable" (ibid.), succinctly articulates the conciliatory aspirations of such filmmaking practices. He is, however, also being somewhat disingenuous about his intentions and we may surmise that the British responded so bitterly to this film because to them its overriding trajectory was to undermine their state institutions, namely the judiciary and the police. The battle lines were drawn up over the issue of the production's tampering with the "truth". Sheridan's finished film not only substantially reworked Conlon's book but also altered the public record in so far as it elided some events and made free with certain characters. Given that *In the Name of the Father* did not proclaim itself to be a docudrama, this might have been unimportant were it not for the lever it gave writers keen to discredit the work's overall message.

Contrary to Sheridan's film, therefore, the Conlons did not share the same cell for any length of time but were often in separate prisons; solicitor Gareth Peirce only entered the case at a late stage; the court case was not heard in the manner portrayed, and much of the legal groundwork was covered by Alistair Logan; Charles Burke was not an elderly tramp but someone Conlon met in a hostel. These "inaccuracies" became the focus of the media's response to the film. For some writers in the broadsheet press, these genuinely detracted from the film's effect. Thus the highly sympathetic film critic in the *Independent on Sunday* hoped that Pete Postlethwaite's performance would "give the English judiciary sleepless nights", as should "the film's presentation of the courtroom, an indictment of the whole adversarial system: its phoney rhetoric . . . absurd pomp and degrading seigneurial judgements". Yet, he still concluded that:

> For all the Guildford Four's importance, Sheridan may have been wiser writing a straight fiction on the imprisoned father and son theme . . . as in Frank McGuinness's play based on the Beirut hostages, *Someone to Watch Over Me*. He might then have made a great film instead of a very good and rousing one. (Curtis, 1994: 25)

Others felt that the focus on the personal and the recourse to melodrama lessened the film's authenticity: "what we get is an emotional spectacle that we're asked to *feel*, without being persuaded to think through, or to ask any questions about" (Romney, 1994: 35: italics in original). These measured critiques were matched elsewhere by an almost hysterical response that was not just restricted to the tabloids. Further, analysis of the film was wrested from the keyboards

of the regular film critics and placed in the hands of columnists, the legal profession and historians. *The Sunday Times*
voiced a fear that was also to arise in connection with *Some
Mother's Son*, that the film's false authenticity would impress
that naïve American audience who would not have the critical tools to see through it:

> Yet, it is its box-office triumph in America, coupled
> with the naïvely uncritical chatshow treatment ac-
> corded Gerry Adams, the Sinn Féin president, that
> has made the film a powerful anti-British propaganda
> tool. For like the young nanny spellbound by *JFK* [the
> article opens with an anecdote about this particular
> simpleton who is heard to comment, on exiting the
> cinema, that the film was based on something that
> really happened] it is particularly an audience en-
> countering a topic for the first time, and ignorant of
> the broad factual outline, that is most prone to ig-
> nore the hazy demarcation between fact and fiction.
> (Millar, 1994: 2)

This kind of critique reminds us that the ideas of the Frank-
furt school still rattle around the critical establishment, little
altered, creating an imaginary hierarchy of viewers from the
informed intelligentsia, capable of deconstructing a text, to
the ignorant proletariat (typically Americans), who are unable to establish any kind of critical distance from the fictions they consume as truths. In fact, the British tabloid
reader was not to remain in ignorance for long as to the
subversive reality of Sheridan's film. An outraged column in
the *Mail on Sunday* by a writer (who confesses not to have
seen the film) reminded them that:

> *In the Name of the Father*, I gather, depicts the police
> (who have all been acquitted of any wrong-doing) as
> ruthless liars, the Government as the enemy and
> concentrates on the story of Gerard Conlon's rela-

> tionship with his father Guiseppe, who died in prison protesting his innocence of involvement with the IRA.
>
> American audiences are fired up even by the trailer — hissing and booing the police and judiciary every time they appear. God knows what will happen when the film is released. (Keane, 1993: 38)

In fact, the writer was able to anticipate what he believed would happen when the film was released — that it would "bring in the biggest cash bonanza the IRA has seen in years" (ibid.). Curiously, none of its detractors seems to consider that the film might arouse local hostility towards the Establishment. There is no sense that it would lend credibility to the IRA campaign amongst Irish immigrants in Britain or that it might further destabilise the situation in Northern Ireland. From this, we may infer that behind all this critical huffing and puffing lay a deeper anxiety about Anglo-American relations, particularly in the wake of Washington's granting of the Adams visa. With a green White House always a threat, and an ineffectual Prime Minister (John Major) representing the nation, any additional support for the IRA, particularly one predicated on a discrediting of the British Establishment, might even further unravel the "special relationship" of the Thatcher/Reagan era. To lend credibility to their case, the broadsheet press annexed Irish columnist, Mary Kenny, to counter, "from the inside", the suggestion that the Irish had a historical grievance against the British:

> Its [*In the Name of the Father*'s] wrongheadedness lies in the political picture it implies. The film opens by presenting the Troubles as a straight struggle between native Irish and the "occupying" British forces. The publicity handouts accompanying the movie even refer to "British occupied Ireland" — unaware, no doubt, as Americans often are, that the term is highly offensive to the majority population in North-

ern Ireland, and that in Ireland itself it is a term primarily used by *An Phoblacht*, the Provisional Sinn Féin newspaper. The flaw in the politics of the film is that at no point is there any allusion — visually, conversationally, or culturally — to the fact that the conflict in the North is not simply a bullying Brits versus victimised Irish line-up: it is essentially about an Orange versus Green tribal quarrel. It is not about "British occupied Ireland": it is about culture and identity. (Kenny, 1993: 18)

The papers also happily reported that *In the Name of the Father* had been criticised by the Maguire family (the Maguire Seven) who claimed not to have been consulted in its making and who objected to being shown at the same trial as the Guildford Four (another inaccuracy). The battle over the film's authenticity was carried as far as its posters; those intended for an American audience carried a sub-heading claiming that the film was "a true story", and when around one hundred of these turned up outside British cinemas, a complaint was registered with the Advertising Standards Authority and the posters were replaced with others reading "Based upon a true story". Before the film's release, there were threats by the Surrey police to sue the filmmakers and their case was taken up by some of the British press who assured their readers that:

> This torture stuff simply could not have happened. Suspects were questioned in the Guildford headquarters, a modern block with ordinary airy offices and windows. There were police officers and civilians in other parts of the building. If prisoners were being ill-treated their screams would have been heard. Early on a doctor examined all suspects. Signs of ill-treatment would have harmed the prosecution case. (Stern and Davis, 1994: 48)

Journalism such as this and that of Keane (above) forms part of a counter-discourse circulating within Britain during this period aimed at casting doubts upon the decision that released the Guildford Four (and by analogy other victims of British judicial misconduct).

This process of vilification was repeated on the release of Some Mother's Son, which was widely condemned as IRA propaganda. It was reported that Helen Mirren's appearance on the National Lottery Live show was cancelled when the BBC saw clips for the film; her place was taken by a Coronation Street star (Harnden, 1997: 2). Indeed, there was much discomfort in the papers over the roles taken by "our" actors, particularly Emma Thompson and Helen Mirren in "anti-British" films. In Northern Ireland, the release of In the Name of the Father was anticipated with concern and it was reported that some cinemas were worried about screening the film because of its political nature, "If I had been offered it seven or eight weeks ago when feelings were running high in the streets [following the bombing of a fish shop in the Shankhill Road and the Greysteel massacre], I would have turned it down," said one cinema manager, "For once the stars are only secondary to the storyline" (McIlwaine, 1993: 1). In the end, this did not occur and the film received either studiously neutral or positive notices. The film critic of the Belfast News Letter was particularly enthusiastic:

> Anyone who takes the time to see In the Name of the Father will find that far from being a propaganda exercise for republican violence it is a clear condemnation of cold-eyed killers within the IRA and their total disregard for "victims of war" wrongly accused of paramilitary plots. And it is a chilling indictment of ruthless policemen not letting the facts stand in the way of a successful prosecution. (Young, 1993: 13)

In contrast with the British media, the American press did indeed embrace *In the Name of the Father* (though history does not reveal whether the film turned moderate Americans into rabid IRA supporters). The *Los Angeles Times* considered it a model of "engaged, enraged filmmaking, a politically charged *Fugitive* [also released that year] that uses one of the most celebrated cases of recent British history to steamroller an audience with the power of rousing, polemical cinema" (Turan, 1993: 1). As this kind of response indicates, the concept of audience manipulation, so derided by the British writers, is considered by critics from within the Hollywood tradition to be a marker of politically engaged cinema. Nor did the same critics have any qualms over embracing the film's truth:

> *In the Name of the Father* makes that familiar situation [an innocent man convicted of a crime he didn't commit] seem almost unbearably disturbing because it tells its true story in such direct, straightforward style. Irish director/co-writer Jim Sheridan . . . understands that the events he re-creates here are horrifying enough that they require no hint of melodramatic hokum. (Medved, 1993: 32)

The redirection of the film's energies from the injustices of the British legal system to the father–son narrative was equally welcomed, most writers commenting approvingly on it:

> *In the Name of the Father* is faithful to the larger facts while taking minor liberties with the Conlons' case, most notably confining both Gerry and Guiseppe in the same prison cell. This shift provides an extraordinary dramatic opportunity for the film to explore the complexities of love between father and son. (Maslin, 1993: 11)

Although a minority of critics found fault with the work on the same grounds as their British counterparts, the consensus was highly favourable. This prompted Conor Cruise O'Brien, who found much to criticise in a film designed to appeal to the "squeamish liberals" of the American upmarket press, to publish an article in *The New Republic* suggesting that *In the Name of the Father* would increase:

> the already significant pressure, originating in the United States and in other parts of the English-speaking world, at several different levels and in several different ways, to bring about British disengagement from Northern Ireland. (Cruise O'Brien, 1999: 314, 313)

This too was the thrust of a similar piece by Richard Grenier (Grenier, 1999), both articles having been written in the light of the lifting of Gerry Adams's visa ban by the Clinton administration. These writers articulate strong anxieties about the "greening" of the White House and Grenier notes the added complication of one of the Guildford Four, Paul Hill's, marriage to Courtney Kennedy, which made him nephew to Senator Edward Kennedy, who supported the Adams visa, and Jean Kennedy Smith, the then US ambassador to Ireland. They may have been justified in their anxieties, since Sheridan has claimed that viewing his film was one of the reasons behind the decision of the White House to grant Adams a visa (Webster, 1988: 88).

The contrasting reception of *In the Name of the Father* in Britain and the United States reflects specific differences both in their film cultures and in levels of political anxiety. By conforming to a Hollywood format, of privileging the personal over the political, Sheridan succeeded in placing his film within the mainstream of American culture. The critics' willingness to "believe" the narrative suggested a familiarity with this kind of filmmaking and indeed, an ability to read political meaning into it. A political message, under these conditions, is only acceptable if accompanied by a personal drama. It was the "knowledge" that these events were "true" that then gave the film its edge. Where the British press apparently worried about the reaction of an ignorant Irish-American audience to the film's "pro-IRA" message, those few critics within the United States who turned their attention to this issue were more anxious about how the film would win friends in high places for the republican cause. What is, perhaps, most extraordinary about these responses was that they were engendered by a single work of art, a modestly budgeted fiction film. Sheridan may not have intended to become a political filmmaker, but it is hard to deny the importance of this film within the political atmosphere of the 1990s.

As McLoone reminds us, *In the Name of the Father*'s controversial reception has tended to deflect attention away from analysis of its performance as a film. The opening sequences, where Gerry evades the army, racing through the narrow alleyways of Belfast to the accompaniment of women beating bin lids, children calling out, and other unknown figures keeping pace with him is, however, exhilarating cinema, suggesting the excitement as well as the menace of life on the streets of Belfast. The appearance of his father, stooped and waving a white handkerchief, further recalls newsreel images of Bloody Sunday. From this point, the action becomes more enclosed, as in contrast with *My Left Foot*, Gerry's world becomes narrower and narrower. A series of two-handers, in which Gerry confronts Guiseppe in the cell, reveal Sheridan's reliance on dialogue to create moments of emotional intensity; yet their wordiness is also crucial to the film's meaning. Words have failed Gerry once, as it is his confession, alongside that of the other members of the Four, which has led not only to his wrongful imprisonment but to that of his father.

Words will be used again in the courtroom to imprison him, their meaninglessness illustrated as the camera shows the defendants ignoring the testimonies and playing hangman amongst themselves. In his early years in prison, his father's words infuriate Gerry who prefers action, rioting in the cell, to Guiseppe's persistent letter writing. Even later, Gerry remains suspicious of language, complaining to Gareth Peirce that he does not have the same command of English that she does. Again, reflecting *My Left Foot*, Gerry's accession to language signals his abandonment of a pre-oedipal lack of self-hood for entry into his father's world. Eventually, he will exchange places with his father, becoming the ailing man's carer and egging him on to live.

In one pivotal scene, the script brings the viewer to the precipice of sentiment before drawing back and recognising its own manipulative power. Guiseppe and Gerry are facing each other in the cell. His father, who is gasping for breath, confides in his son that, "Every night, I take your mother's hand in mine. We go out the front door, into Cypress Street, down the Falls Road, up the Antrim Road, to Cave Hill; we look back down on poor troubled Belfast. I've been doing that every night for five years now as if I never left your mother." Gerry responds, "What I remember most about my childhood is my wee hand in your big hand. And the smell of tobacco. I remember I could smell the tobacco off the palm of your hand. When I want to feel happy, I try to remember the smell of tobacco." Guiseppe gasps, "Hold my hand" to which his son replies with an explosion of laughter, "Get the fuck . . . Don't go sentimental on me now." If the use of language is a political statement, a constant source of tension between oppressor and oppressed, nevertheless, in the right conditions it allows for an expression of emotion that is more salutary than violence.

The intensely emotive scenes between father and son have, as we have already discussed, the effect of deflecting attention from the central source of friction, the determination of the British authorities to try to convict the Guildford Four and Maguire Seven, and subsequently to cover up this miscarriage of justice. Yet the focus on individuals rather than processes, whilst it may result in an emotional rather than a politically informed response, is a classic cinematic device for engaging audience identification and sympathy. Just as the popular press will always pursue the human element of any headline story, so popular cinema goes for the heart over the head. It was, of course, this tactical manipulation that so incensed the film's detractors and the ensuing war of media words is indicative of the battle for hegemony that took place around the film's meaning. This debacle illustrates the susceptibility of any text to the interpretative process. For as much as Sheridan weighed in before and after the event (of the film's release) in an attempt to influence readings of *In the Name of the Father*, so other competing voices clamoured for the superiority of their analyses of its meaning and message.

Certainly, *In the Name of the Father* became *ipso facto* a political film; whether or not its textual construction conforms to a model of political filmmaking is probably only answerable in the context of a wider debate about the nature of entertainment cinema. As a text, it is far more effective than *Some Mother's Son* in articulating a clear position and in a manner that offers the audience a point of insertion into the dramatic action. Within the tradition of popular cinema, it demands to be recognised as injecting an array of local concerns into a popular, universal format in a manner that few other contemporary Irish films have achieved.

Chapter Four

The Boxer (1997):
The Performance of Peace

Jim Sheridan has said that he made *The Boxer* "as a reaction to *In the Name of the Father*" (see interview). Undoubtedly, the media circus that engulfed the release of his Guildford Four film left him reluctant to run the gauntlet again with another controversial work. Tempted as he may have been to make "a commercial American film" (ibid.), and we can be sure he was not short of offers, he decided instead to pursue his exploration of the Troubles this time as a straightforward fiction film. Teaming up again with Terry George as co-scriptwriter, Sheridan proceeded to make his most overtly generic work, a boxing drama starring Daniel Day-Lewis.

The resulting film met with a much happier media response but less rewarding box-office figures. In Ireland, it took about €1,016,000, a significant drop on Sheridan's previous films (Barton, 2001: 31), and in the US it grossed just $4.8 million in its first month, having cost $40 million to make (Doyle, 1998: 4). It performed equally badly in the UK. There are a number of probable causes for this somewhat disappointing income, both at home and overseas. The most apparent one is an *ennui* with films about the Troubles. With a few exceptions, the most obvious being *In the Name of the*

Father, works that have attempted to engage with the events of the last 30 years have failed to find a large audience. This does not just apply to film, but to the arts in general. Ronan Bennett has suggested that the middle classes in Northern Ireland have had little involvement with the Troubles and do not expect that the cultural artefacts they patronise should deal with local political issues; whilst only local community groups such as the West Belfast Community Festival have commissioned and promoted politically engaged art forms (Bennett, 1998). In terms of cinema, the lack of interest shown by the various bodies who might be expected to fund local productions has meant that, until recently, there has been essentially no indigenous, contemporary Northern Irish feature filmmaking.

As we shall be discussing below, the advent of the peace process, combined with a variety of new funding opportunities, has resulted in a greater filmic engagement with life in Northern Ireland as a whole. Viewer apathy, however, remains a disincentive. In the Republic, the situation is little different, with Sheridan remaining one of the few Southern filmmakers to have returned to Northern Irish subject matter. Nor have audiences in Britain and the US shown any consistent or informed interest in works about the Troubles; indeed, the opposite is closer to the truth.

An additional disincentive has been the inability of filmmakers to break with the conventions of representation. We saw in the previous chapter how most indigenous filmmakers have been constrained by the imperative of achieving a balanced view, whilst condemning acts of violence. Thus, paramilitaries have been consistently depicted as psychopaths acting without the consent of their community (a view that is inconsistent with history) or good people unwillingly trapped in a conflict for which there is no exit other than death. The paradigms for this discursive cul-de-sac were, as John Hill has illustrated in his classic analysis of representations of violence (Hill, 1987; also McLoone, 2000), established by British filmmakers conforming to expectations that IRA activities should be seen as arising out of a natural Irish proclivity for irrational violence. The alternative explanation, that the Irish had a justifiable grievance based on a history of colonisation and economic exclusion, was evidently inconceivable. The continuing reluctance of filmmakers to take a new look at the causes of violence has resulted in a representational void. The same signifiers of the Troubles recur in film after film: hovering helicopters, blacked-up soldiers, rundown inner-city streets, scurrying civilians, and lurking terrorists. The ubiquity of these images has rendered them meaningless; they are simply local colour, a "cut-and-paste" background against which a more engaging narrative must be placed in order to draw in an audience.

Filmmakers wishing to reflect on the Troubles in a realistic manner have also had to negotiate the question of censorship. Most will opt for self-censorship, as Terry George's response to Andy White's criticism of *Some Mother's Son* (see previous chapter) suggests:

> Hey, Andy, of course you're right that we didn't show the shards of glass in schoolgirls' faces or the dismembered bodies of soldiers, nor did we show the blanket protesters being wire-brushed clean, or the maggots and lice in the cells, or the innumerable atrocities committed by each side against the other; but then, *Some Mother's Son* is a film. And films have boundaries, and in your case the boundary, according to the Irish censor Seamus Smith, was a couple of swearwords and two shootings.
>
> That was enough for him to give us an over-18 certificate (a decision reduced by the Appeal Board). Can you imagine if we'd have included the shards of glass and the guts you so crave for [*sic*]? We might have been banned! (George, 1996: 15)

The response of the British media to Irish films that appear to have a republican bias has already been discussed. When these include high levels of explicit violence, as did another Troubles film, *Resurrection Man* (Marc Evans, UK, 1997), adapted by Eoin McNamee from his novel of the same name, then the reaction can be even more antagonistic. *Resurrection Man* ran the critical gauntlet for its "sick" treatment of the real-life Shankhill Butchers, a loyalist gang that operated in the 1970s and was responsible for a number of random knifings, skinnings and beatings, directed primarily at Catholics but also involving fellow loyalists. McNamee has since claimed that, "The Tory press in England lost their heads over it — 'a poisonous outpouring of anti-Unionist bile by Irish writer Eoin McNamee' — and it was effectively censored out of existence" (Wallace, 2001: 6).

Under such conditions, the formula most favoured by filmmakers in search of a narrative structure for Troubles cinema has been the "love-across-the-divide" story. Films such as *Cal* (Pat O'Connor, GB, 1984), *The Crying Game* (Neil Jordan, UK, 1992), *Nothing Personal* (Thaddeus O'Sullivan, Ireland, 1995) and *This is the Sea* (Mary McGuckian, Ireland/USA/GB, 1996), feature a central love story between two symbolic protagonists. In McGuckian's film, for instance, the romance is between a Protestant girl, brought up in a rural community that recalls the Amish setting of Peter Weir's similarly themed *Witness* (Peter Weir, US, 1985), and a Catholic boy from an economically deprived area. Set against the background of the 1994 ceasefire, it charts the resistance of the Protestant family to the idea of their daughter having a Catholic boyfriend. Over-schematic to an almost ludicrous point, it eventually unites its lovers only after a narrative of personal tragedy and loss. In this, it could be said to be more optimistic for the coming-together of the two sides in the divide than its predecessors, notably *Cal* and *Nothing Personal*. In his analysis of a selection of these "love-across-the-divide" stories, Joe Cleary has written that the inevitable failure of the two lovers to be united sets them apart from the general run of national romances:

> It is as if this romance mode has been called into be-ing by the Northern Irish situation as an attempt to imagine "resolutions" to it, but in the face of the conflict's intractability, which stems from the ab-sence of any agreed-upon state order that might frame a political solution acceptable to both sides, the utopian impulse of the romance mode must give way to a "realism" shorn of any such transformative impetus. (Cleary, 1996: 241)

The tendency of "love-across-the-divide" narratives to see that divide as being a loyalist/republican one, aligns them with the "two tribes" analysis of the Troubles, again to the detriment of any suggestion that republican paramilitary ac-tivity has been aimed at the representatives of the British political order, primarily the army, but also members of the security forces. This schematic viewpoint further militates against any analysis of class or other social factors. An alter-native formula has been to locate IRA activists within the wider frame of the terrorist genre. Thus, a number of Hollywood films feature IRA killers as demented assassins with a mission to subvert western democracy. We have al-ready mentioned, in Chapter Two, Sean Bean's virtual re-prise of his role as psychopath terrorist in *Patriot Games* (where he is an IRA man) and *GoldenEye* (where he is not). Some of the more unlikely actors to portray killer IRA men on the run include Brad Pitt in *The Devil's Own* (Alan J. Pakula, US, 1997), and Richard Gere as a particularly sympa-thetic hitman in *The Jackal* (Michael Caton-Jones, US, 1997). Such films make little pretence of engaging with the political motivation of the republican military campaign, and, indeed, are generally at pains to explain to audiences that their IRA protagonists are renegades who do not represent the wider aims of the organisation.

The Boxer is essentially a "love-across-the-divide" tale, with the difference that in this instance the divide is an internal one, between the old guard of the IRA that is, the film suggests, still entrenched in violence, and the supporters of the peace process. It opens with soundbites from the peace process, the disembodied voices of Clinton, Blair and Paisley commenting on the negotiations. The section ends ominously with Ian Paisley saying, "It hasn't gone away, you know." As images and the titles begin to appear on the screen, the opening sequences counterpoint Danny Flynn's (Daniel Day-Lewis) release from prison with the jail wedding of an IRA prisoner and the celebrations (in his absence) afterwards. Two contrasting sets of associations instantly emerge from these scenes: Danny is shot as a solitary figure against a background of cold greys and blues; the community from which the prisoner and his wife are drawn is visualised as washed in a golden-reddish light, suggesting simultaneously warmth and enclosure as well as a certain garishness. The guests mill around the bride's family at the party, songs are sung and rituals revisited. A sense of entrapment is swiftly established when a young man dances with another prisoner's wife; for this he is threatened with a kneecapping by the older men and scolded ferociously by his mother.

That this is an ageing community caught in stasis is further underlined in Danny's first visit to his former boxing club. Now closed down, it is presented as a dusty, unused space, partially lit by shafts of sunlight that pick out the old men who still linger on there. An elegiac soundtrack reinforces the sense of decay, filtered with nostalgia for times past. Soon after this scene, an encounter between the local IRA leader, Joe Hamill (Brian Cox) and his bitter lieutenant, Harry (Gerard McSorley) introduces the film's pivotal conflict: Hamill informs Harry that a ceasefire will commence the following day; the latter pronounces it a sell-out. His personal motivations for opposing the ceasefire are revealed when his wife derides it as a betrayal of what their son died for. The Juliet to Danny's Romeo is Hamill's daughter, Maggie (Emily Watson). His childhood girlfriend, she married Danny's best friend after Danny was imprisoned for unspecified IRA activity. Her husband is now doing time, leaving her with a young teenage son, Liam (Ciarán Fitzgerald).

Danny returns to his old flat, his old boxing club, retrieves his old trainer, Ike (Ken Stott) from alcoholic oblivion and sets out to restore his boxing reputation. Under Ike's management, the Holy Family Boxing Club is reestablished along its traditional non-sectarian lines and, in keeping with the new spirit of the ceasefire, Ike accepts equipment donated for publicity purposes from the RUC. Some sections of the IRA, however, are not ready for such gestures; nor is Liam prepared for Danny to take his father's place and in the wake of street riots, Liam and his friends set fire to the club, which is destroyed. Danny leaves to fight in London but returns to Maggie, and Ike is assassinated after exchanging words with Harry. The film ends with a showdown in which Hamill's men kill Harry and Danny appears to be united with Maggie.

Within the body of Sheridan's work, *The Boxer* is unusual on a number of counts. It lacks much of the teleological drive of the other films, and its resolution is particularly indeterminate. The opening sequences establish beyond doubt that the status of the prisoner's wife is little different to that of her incarcerated husband. We learn little about Maggie's husband, except that, with small hope of an early release programme for IRA prisoners, he is unlikely to come home. Liam ultimately accepts Danny as a surrogate father but with little narrative basis, other than the fact that he is a charismatic boxer. The suggestion that Maggie and Danny will be able to overcome community hostility to the "unfaithful" prison wife is therefore hardly credible within the larger framework of the film. Both make it clear that Belfast is their home and that leaving it for another territory, say America, is not an option. Even leaving the Catholic side of the barricades for the Protestant sector is demonstrated to be a naïve exercise as they are both instantly marked as intruders. They can only achieve a small measure of romantic union when they go to the seaside, which merely revisits a conventional trope within Irish cinema — escape from the unfree space of the metropolis to the spiritually as well as physically open countryside.

On a symbolic level, this inability to achieve a convincing narrative closure reflects the film's own anxieties about the feasibility of the peace process. On an artistic level, it remains somewhat unsatisfactory. In itself, the introduction of a love-story element into the narrative marks another departure for Sheridan. Certainly, *My Left Foot* ended on a romantic note, but this functioned as little more than a coda to the main narrative. In the other films, heterosexual love is jettisoned in favour of working through their oedipal concerns. In *The Boxer*, these now have to compete with the central love affair.

Father-figures remain crucial to the film's construction, though it could be said that they also contribute to its somewhat opaque meaning. From the position of the son in *My Left Foot* and *In the Name of the Father*, Daniel Day-Lewis now plays the symbolic father to Liam and the other hopefuls he is training. Liam must choose between Danny as good father and his biological father, who, as an unrepentant IRA prisoner, the film propels into the role of bad father. Here it finds itself backed into an epistemological corner, since we know little about Maggie's husband other than that he was Danny's best friend. Maggie appears to have decided to leave him and the film seems to endorse this. However, morally and generically, this position is untenable. The kind of

Hollywood narratives that this film emulates simply would not endorse such unmotivated marital infidelity; nor is it easy to imagine how Maggie and Danny could continue to live in Catholic West Belfast and hold on to their relationship. The good father/bad father duality is refracted back onto the older generation with the juxtaposition of Harry and Joe Hamill, both "godfathers" to the community and parents themselves. Harry, it is suggested, passed on his contaminated republicanism to his son, causing his death; Joe Hamill fathered a daughter whom love and biological destiny impels to embrace a peaceful future.

Although Sheridan has alluded to his ambition to make an Irish love story (see interview), he appears to have, for him, unusual difficulty in directing his actors' love-scenes. Nor does he ever manage to integrate Maggie fully into the boxing narrative. On the other hand, the film betrays a much stronger sense of cinema as a visual medium than Sheridan's previous works. It remains wordy, the background to the central love-affair being sketched in through a sequence of somewhat contrived scenes where Maggie and Danny recount to each other how they met. The introductory sequences, however, where Danny's release is juxtaposed with the prison wedding, and in which Danny and Ike return to the abandoned boxing club, achieve their meaning through recourse to the visual and aural rather than through dialogue.

Veteran cinematographer, Chris Menges, who was also responsible for Neil Jordan's *Angel* (Ireland, 1982) and *Michael Collins* (US, 1996), as well as *The Killing Fields* (Roland Joffé, UK, 1984), *The Mission* (Roland Joffé, UK, 1986), and many others, appears to have been given considerable scope to create a sense of entrapment in time and place by means of a visual language. Repeated shots of hostile onlookers and the final intrusive presence of the helicopter suggests paranoia and a failure of privacy, underlined by the spatial layout of Maggie and her father's home, where burly IRA henchmen crowd the small rooms, frisking even Maggie as she goes back and forth. Harry's wife's wordless anguish when she cradles her murdered husband, thug that the film has established him to be, recalls the pieta pose even as it relegates her to the inevitable marker of female/universal suffering.

Like many films set in Belfast, *The Boxer* was in fact shot in Dublin; this partly explains the film's lack of any specific geographical anchor. This, and the film's recourse to the conventional signifiers of Troubles Belfast annoyed at least one local critic who complained that "the fault in the film lies in the tired re-working of old sores, a parade of depressingly clichéd figures and a total lack of the feel and atmosphere of Belfast (setting a film in one city and shooting it in another simply never works)" (*The Irish News*, 1998: 13).

The decision to utilise a well-established genre format, the boxing movie, marks another departure. Sheridan has said that "Daniel wanted to make a boxing film" (see interview), and he took this opportunity to graft onto it a message about renouncing violence. Although the previous films had largely conformed to Hollywood formulae in terms of their overall construction, they had only made loose concessions to recognisable generic features, notably, in the case of *In the Name of the Father*, to the prison thriller and the courtroom drama.

The boxing film brings with it an array of generic concerns, principally to do with codes of honour and masculinity. The conventional narrative of such films has a young man from the wrong side of the tracks break out of his social milieu through his dedication to, and flair for, boxing. Once he has made it, the trappings of wealth will inevitably tempt him, and his acceptance into his new social background will be signalled by his rejection of his small-time girlfriend or wife. At the same time, the shady interests that run the gambling networks behind the fighting will now increasingly pressurise the naïve hero to make them more money; this

usually involves "throwing" a match, letting a lesser opponent win in order that the gamblers on the inside will clean
up against the odds. This decision will bring into question his
integrity and force him to confront the compromises he has
had to make in order to cross the line between anonymity
and success. Such, for instance, is the storyline that structures *The Set-Up* (Robert Wise, US, 1948) and *Raging Bull*
(Martin Scorsese, US, 1980). The genre reached its widest
audience with the succession of *Rocky* films made between
1976 and 1990 by John G. Avildsen and Sylvester Stallone.
These stripped-down fables reduced boxing to its essentials,
each one outdoing the last in its iconising of the beauty and
brutality of the game.

Central to these films, and others such as Raoul Walsh's
Gentleman Jim (US, 1942) is their fascination with masculinity, the male body and the masochistic pleasure of contact
sport. The ring is elevated in the boxing film to the specular
site of masculinity as performance; violence is alternatively
redemptive and excessive. In *Raging Bull*, Jake La Motta
moves within a world where masculinity is a privileged discourse and the brutal treatment of women a given. As his
body ages and fattens in a process that became part of the
film's extra-diegetic existence (with publicity handouts
drawing attention to the star, Robert de Niro's, weight gain
for the film), so the real and the performative merge. In the
final sequences of Scorsese's work, a puffed-up La Motta
sits at his stage mirror, preparing to perform as his earlier
self in front of the tawdry audience that now pays to see
him, by rehearsing the words of another fictional boxer
who threw a game, Marlon Brando's Terry Malloy: "I
could'a' been a contender . . .".

Daniel Day-Lewis's own preparation for the film, under
the tutelage of former world boxing champion, Barry
McGuigan, drew parallels in the press between his and de
Niro's commitment to method acting. Day-Lewis allegedly

trained obsessively for three years, breaking his nose and injuring his back in the process. He is rewarded in the film with three fight sequences, of which the final is shot in the classic slow-motion style of the boxing drama and accompanied by heightened sound-effects of thudding bodies.

If, however, the point of the boxing film is to explore the obsessive nature of sporting commitment and to question the demarcation between the spectacle of violence and its enactment in the everyday articulation of masculinity, then *The Boxer*, by its nature as a Troubles film, can only partly accede to generic expectations. For a start, Danny's single-minded engagement with the sport is diluted by the love-story which he must pursue with equal diligence if less conviction. He is, on the one hand, the classic existential loner, a familiar archetype of Hollywood cinema.

On the other, he is the bearer of the symbolic love affair that will cement the community and reinvent the family. By positioning himself outside of society, he invites the audience to share his alienated gaze at the civil disturbances around him. He has renounced whatever tenuous connection he had with the IRA (this remains unexplained, although we know he took the rap for Harry and didn't "talk" in jail) and embraced peace. "I'm not a killer, Maggie," he tells his lover, "but this place makes me want to kill." This is born out by his refusal to beat his opponent in the London ring to pulp, a gesture that loses him the fight. Like his other roles in Sheridan's films, Daniel Day-Lewis's Danny is a gentle individual for whom aggression is performative rather than natural. That "this place" makes Danny want to kill reflects a commonly held interpretation of the Troubles as a part of the social fabric of working class Northern Irish life.

This deterministic point of view is reflected in the stand-off between Harry and Joe Hamill. Harry, as played by Gerard McSorley, is entrapped within his own rhetoric; like the prisoner's bride, it makes little difference whether he is

inside or outside of jail. He is personally motivated to continue to fight by the need to justify the death of his own son,
aged 13, when taking part in paramilitary activities that Ike
says were futile. As a role, it could have veered into the
IRA-man-as-psychopath archetype mentioned above, but
McSorley's performance anchors it on the side of the tragic.
Given such opposition, it is hard to see how Hamill's reasoned and world-weary approach to negotiation can suc-
ceed. The solution, to assassinate Harry, hardly suggests a
universal formula. What, then, is the film's message?

    In part, it is about the nature of violence, in particular
the distinction between aggression (boxing) and violence
(paramilitary activities). To appreciate the dynamics of this
discourse, it is necessary to understand the specific place of
boxing within Northern Irish society. The film originated in a
biography of Barry McGuigan written by Jim Sheridan, *Leave
the Fighting to McGuigan* (Viking, 1985). McGuigan is himself a
symbolic figure within Northern Irish culture. He comes
from Clones in County Monaghan, one of the three counties
that is in the province of Ulster but located within the Republic of Ireland. He is from a Catholic family and married to
a Protestant. His manager, Barney Eastwood, persuaded
McGuigan that his best interests lay in competing within the
British boxing circuit and his image was carefully cultivated
to appeal to Protestants as well as Catholics. His major
fights took place in an arena stripped of national flags of any
hue. The decision to play his father's recording of "Danny
Boy" at his fights in the place of either national anthem was
all part of the same strategy of de-politicisation. This, however, was viewed as a sell-out by members of the nationalist
community and his triumphant tour of Belfast after winning
the world title was marred by an outbreak of slogans daubed
on walls that read, "Barry the Brit — sold his soul for English gold" (Sugden and Harvie, 1995: 135). Similarly, when
Wayne McCullough, a Protestant from Belfast's Shankhill

Road, carried the Irish tricolour in the Seoul Olympics as part of the All-Ireland boxing team, his home was besieged by protestors.

These displays of sectarianism reflect the peculiar history of boxing in the North with which the Holy Family club, featured in *The Boxer*, is intricately linked. Sugden and Harvie, in their brief history of the sport, note that it was the British army that helped lay the foundations of amateur boxing in Belfast, prior to the Troubles, when Belfast was a garrison town. Another significant contributor to the tradition was the police force, initially as the Royal Irish Constabulary (RIC) and subsequently, after partition, under its new guise as the Royal Ulster Constabulary (RUC) (ibid.: 126–35). If these two groups institutionalised the sport, they were only putting a formal stamp on what had been a popular activity since the early nineteenth century. Outside the ring, the tradition of bare-fisted street fighting was central to the culture of the Belfast working class, both Catholic and Protestant, before the ascendancy of the paramilitary regime.

Allen Feldman has gathered together and analysed reminiscences about these men that describe the replacement of the "hardman" (boxer) by the gunman. Where the former was motivated by the performative quality of violence, the local status of fame, and the exhilaration of one-to-one conflict, the latter was viewed as part of a unit, an extension of the mechanical (the gun), and necessarily anonymous. Similarly, the former was non-political and functioned within the rules established by the community, the latter highly politicised and occupying an ambiguous relationship with the community. Feldman further argues that:

> The era of the hardman coincided with the cultural dominance of industrial capitalism in Belfast. The hardman fights and its locales and characters were central to the iconography of industrial working-class

culture. The hardman ethic was a revaluation of the
body confronted with the power of the machine, not
an unusual response considering the relatively recent
rural background of the Belfast labor force in the first
half of this century. This ethic valorized both physical
performance and the moral construction of the body
through rules of performance. (Feldman, 1991: 56)

In the last century, boxing clubs were established both by
the Catholic Church and as offshoots of Protestant factories
or youth clubs. The high level of unemployment in both
communities, but particularly amongst working-class Catholics, gave rise to the conditions that Sugden and Harvie agree
are essential to the organic growth of boxing as a sport:

the boxing subculture is sustained by a mixture of
aggressive masculinity; the capacity of the sport to
provide a positively sanctioned channel for this trait;
and the belief that the sport can offer a form of sanctuary from urban poverty and related social problems. (Sugden and Harvie, 1995: 128)

Although the amateur boxing clubs drew their fighters from
the community within which they were located, competition
between both sides of the divide was maintained throughout
the Troubles. Furthermore, successful clubs in Catholic areas attracted boxers from the Protestant side in search of
the superior facilities and coaching on offer:

In the case of the Holy Family Boxing Club, in the
Catholic New Lodge estate, the clientele are actually
mixed, with young boxers from areas with radically
different political reputations training and fighting
side by side each night of the week, supervised by
trainers and coaches from both sides of the sectarian
divide. (ibid.: 130)

Once again, we can see how Sheridan drew on historical fact which he then transformed into a popular, fictionalised narrative. Initially, he had planned to make a film about McGuigan but this gradually metamorphosed into the version that became *The Boxer*. The strict divisions between boxing and paramilitary violence that exist within Northern Ireland are essential to the film's wider message. On the one side, there is Danny whose physical prowess reinvigorates the community; on the other, Harry whose anonymous execution of paramilitary violence (we never see him actually kill Ike or plant the bomb that will explode on the night of Danny's fight) draws on different codes of honour.

In a more subtle way, the film further destabilises the traditional interpretation of the Troubles as reflecting a native proclivity for violence. Through its insistence on the separation of the hardman and the gunman, it validates a historical and regional pleasure in fighting as a sport which it posits as radically distinct from terrorist engagement. In fact, it was from this tradition of bare-fisted street fighting, which emigrants brought to their new communities, that the stereotype of the "fighting Irish" emerged. This institutionalised violence, far from inciting "tribal hatreds" is, in the film, the catalyst for bringing together the two communities after many years of separation. In a somewhat contrived sequence, Ike calls out the names of members of the club from both religious traditions who have died as a result of the Troubles, the camera picking out their parents as he speaks. "Sentimental shite," Harry intones in response, remarking later to Danny, "It's not just boxing, Danny. It's a fucking statement." Indeed, Sugden and Harvie would probably be more likely to agree with Harry's analysis of this scene than Ike or Danny's. They point out that the individual nature of boxing means that any rejection of sectarianism implicit in the boxer's decision to compete and train with members of the other community makes little overall difference:

Along with a decision to become a serious boxer comes an implicit rejection of many of the degrading aspects of life in Belfast including terrorism and the subculture which sustains boundless violence.

Also, the more successful a serious boxer is in his career the more opportunity he will have to travel and experience longer term relationships with people of different religious, racial and national backgrounds. However, the individual fighter's rejection of the sectarianism and boundless violence which may be characteristic of certain areas of his home town has little impact on the underpinning structure of cross-community conflict there. The most likely result of a serious fighter from Belfast having his horizons broadened through involvement in boxing is that he will move house. (Sugden and Harvie, 1995: 133)

Sheridan's film *is* a statement, a call to forsake political violence for constitutional politics and for a return to a non-sectarian community life based around certain shared pleasures, such as sport. The threat to such a utopian future is, in this vista, the recalcitrance of those members of the IRA who remain wedded to the armalite rather than the ballot-box. Such a message could not but redeem the filmmaker in the eyes of the British press. They fastened on *The Boxer* with gusto: "Can you take another film about boxing? Can you take another film about Northern Ireland? You can. You will" read the *Guardian* review (Williams, 1998: 3). The critic concedes that "it may simply be a very good film, rather than a great one", but:

I came out of it feeling that hardly ever do you see a movie so carefully and honestly analysing the complexity of conflict, so intelligent in its exposure of the roots of evil acts, so unwilling to cut emotional corners. (ibid.)

It was placed at Number Two in the Critic's Choice listings in the same newspaper and awarded four stars (over Neil Jordan's *The Butcher Boy*, which was relegated to the three-star category). The other critics concurred and, on this occasion, when an Irish guest columnist was invited to offer an "informed" local perspective on the film, the response was equally positive. Eoghan Harris penned a lengthy article in *The Sunday Times* arguing that:

> A remarkable new film, *The Boxer*, is set to blow British and Irish audiences out of their political apathy about the North. . . . What makes it remarkable is that it is the first balanced film on Northern Ireland for almost 15 years, and a model of how to meld politics and drama that film-makers tackling Northern Ireland have too often ignored. (Harris, 1998: 2)

This elevation of balance over polemics was largely felt to distinguish this film from Sheridan's and George's two preceding films. However, the absence of any representation of the British establishment must surely have lain at the heart of the film's appeal to critics and columnists within the British media. The suggestion that *The Boxer* got to the roots of the conflict similarly reflects a sense of relief over issues of liability. Violence and destruction are explained in the film as motivated largely by personal, familial causes. Harry must justify the death of his son; Liam wants to avenge his absent father. The main political reason given for opposing the ceasefires is that the release of prisoners has not been guaranteed, although Harry also recalls the death of the hunger strikers and wonders what they died for. However, the IRA's lack of faith in the real desire of the British government to pursue negotiations, a lack of faith based on historical precedent, remains an unexplored theme.

The only instance where the film engages with the British dimension to Northern Irish life is when it has Danny go to London to box for money. His opponent is, symbolically, a Nigerian, another victim of Empire and the neo-colonial world-order, in which the former colonial powers retain economic control over territories they have vacated. English boxing circles are lampooned as venial and shallow, signalled by glitzy women and a waiter who requests of the noisy Irish contingent that they "confine their appreciation to clapping". This scene has little diegetic weight other than to reinforce Danny's decision that he cannot leave Belfast, as it is his home. It also serves as a reminder of how little explored the economic background to the film remains. Only the visual recreation of Belfast as a post-industrial space suggests that the performance of masculinity within the framework of terrorism may correspond to the economic disempowerment of the male members of the community. None of the film's main protagonists appears to have a job or occupation other than terrorism. Boxing thus provides an alternative mode of validating the physical prowess of the male body.

The film's balance was also lauded in the Irish press, who seemed equally unconcerned about its privileging of emotion over analysis; in the Republic, *The Boxer* was widely welcomed as a relief from the stereotyping process that was seen to have hindered a more insightful treatment of the Troubles. Writing in *The Irish Times,* the playwright, Gary Mitchell echoed this opinion from a Northern Protestant perspective:

> Each argument [for and against the ceasefire] is given a healthy portion of respect; and when the non-violent supporters use violence to win the argument, the irony and complexity of schisms within nationalism are suitably demonstrated. All this political intrigue is embellished by believable and recognisable characters and rounded off with the complicated love triangle between the ex-prisoner Danny and a prisoner's wife. You are left with a definite feeling

that in the Catholic/nationalist community you have
both good and bad. (Mitchell, 1998: 13)

The film's apparent viewpoint that the achievement of peace
was solely a matter of the IRA renouncing violence equally
endeared it to the (Protestant) _Belfast Telegraph_'s reviewer:

> This is Sheridan's best film since his stunning debut.
> He's a political film-maker and since then he became
> increasingly fixated with Northern politics, the
> Troubles and human rights — with mixed results.
>
> In collaboration with writer Terry George, there has
> been _In The Name of the Father_ and George's morally
> unmanageable _Some Mother's Son_. Now it's as if
> Sheridan has reached a new maturity, a coming of
> age which recognises peace in Northern Ireland is
> the only way forward.
>
> Somewhere, some mother's son may describe this
> film as anti-IRA. Well now, that's a surprise. Cer-
> tainly it accepts with a grim resignation that Catho-
> lics and Protestants must live together if there is to
> be a future . . . and it is the IRA hawk in the cast
> who falls to his doom screeching the old hatreds . . .
> but it is a film that confronts the pain and torment of
> Ulster. It hurts emotionally, it moves, it disturbs,
> and, most of all perhaps, it discomforts, no easy an-
> swers, no rest for the wicked. (Hunter, 1998: 12)

Disappointment over the film's reluctance to probe the political issues surrounding the ceasefires, or perhaps its lack of
anti-Britishness, was largely confined to the American press.
Whilst the reviews were modestly enthusiastic in the main,
the film was generally seen to be an anticlimax after _In the
Name of the Father_. The _Time_ magazine critic articulated this
sense of disappointment when he wrote that, "The mass
audience has paid scant attention to films about the Irish
Troubles, but this one may find friends precisely because it

renounces political nuance for emotional bullying and old Hollywood-style blarney." Conceding the potency of "cheap movies", he suggests that:

> Jim Sheridan . . . may have figured that subtlety has no place in a story about the lunatic fervor of Irish extremist politics. Or maybe he figured his cast could make the gritty fantasy plausible. Day-Lewis very nearly does. (Corliss, 1998: 84)

Corliss, in fact, was wrong as the mass audience did not embrace *The Boxer*, despite its "soft" romantic centre — but few films could compete with the alternative viewing at that time, another "Irish" story, James Cameron's *Titanic* (US, 1997).

The desire to view Sheridan's film as balanced reflects the political aspirations of the time. It also demonstrates a need to find some template that will result in a more engaged filmic treatment of the issues at stake. In their rush, therefore, to laud *The Boxer*, these critics forget that the "Hawk and Dove" formula has long been pivotal to cinema's dramatic treatment of Northern Ireland and the IRA. The good IRA man / bad IRA man duality structures one of the canonical films of British cinema's Northern Ireland cycle, *The Gentle Gunman* (Basil Dearden, UK, 1952) in which two brothers (played by Dirk Bogarde and John Mills) function as symbolic representatives of reason versus emotion, with a shadowy IRA leader, Shinto (Robert Beatty) urging them on to excessive acts of violence that will destroy the family of their disputed girlfriend. *Shake Hands with the Devil*, mentioned in Chapter Three, is similarly themed.

Nor can it be really argued that the film's message is balanced, since it clearly comes down on the side of negotiation. Even though there is an air of the tragic about Harry, the fact that it is suggested that he is responsible for the callous murder of Ike, whose body is dumped on city wasteground, ultimately leaves little room for compassion towards

him. Joe Hamill, on the other hand, is the world-weary sen-
ior statesman concerned for his daughter's wellbeing and
protective of his grandson. He is flexible in his attitudes, as
we are shown when he is reconciled to Danny and Maggie's
love, but he also has access to considerable power. Balance,
in this terminology, equates with criticism of the anti-peace
process wing of the IRA and its offshoot members.

A number of films made in the wake of the peace process
(of 1993 onwards), explore the viewpoint that some kind of
closure might be achievable. Many also try to encompass a
wider range of representations. These include attempts to
see the Troubles from the viewpoint of loyalist paramilitaries
(*Nothing Personal*), and of women who were drawn in to violence (*Bogwoman,* Tom Collins, GB/Ireland/ Germany, 1997),
as well as remembering those such as the "Peace People"
who tried to achieve peace in an earlier era (*Titanic Town*
(Roger Michell, UK/Germany/France, 1998)).

The other consequence of the peace process, combined
with some internal television funding, has been a desire to
move away from representations of the Troubles altogether
and explore the wider dynamics of Northern Irish society.
The best of the resulting productions have been short films
for television, such as *The Cake* (Jo Neylin, Ireland, 1995) and
the Oscar-nominated *Dance, Lexie, Dance* (Tim Loane, UK,
1996). Less has been seen of this movement in feature filmmaking, though the marital comedy, *With or Without You* (Michael Winterbottom, UK/US, 1999) is set in a remarkably
hip Belfast that makes the city look like Anytown, UK, on a
sunny day. As John Hill has written of such films:

> While a number of the features have continued to
> be "Troubles" dramas, displaying varying degrees of
> originality in their representation of the conflicts,
> many of the shorts have sought to break out of the
> "Troubles" paradigm, either by attending to other

> matters or seeking to render problematic the tradi-
> tional binaries — British and Irish, Protestant and
> Catholic — that have conventionally structured per-
> ceptions of Northern Ireland life. (Hill, 1999: 27)

With the promise of an end to violence never quite fulfilling itself, "peace process" films, such as *The Boxer*, have ulti-mately found themselves foundering within a milieu of politi-cal uncertainty. In interview, Sheridan and others involved in its making have described how this instability fed in to the film, and in particular how the "shifting ground" of the peace process, in Daniel Day-Lewis's words, "has us over an anvil. We have a responsibility to what is happening right at this moment" (Webster, 1998: 101). These uncertainties, com-bined with the need to make films for as wide as possible an audience, have resulted in works that still tend to deal in universal themes whilst attempting to integrate a political message into their story lines. They are not so much taking the specific and rendering it universal, as do the IRA-man-as-international-terrorist films, but taking the universal and rendering it specific.

Within this filmmaking category, *The Boxer* exemplifies the latter approach. It deploys a recognisable generic format, which it furnishes with two stars that can provide an inter-national reputation and strong acting performances. It then proceeds to inject into this formula a specific message — the need to engage in dialogue rather than continue to pur-sue a path of violence — and works this up to the extent that its primary generic narrative is in danger of being sub-sumed by its "local" politics. Finally, faced with an increasing lack of confidence in the outcome of its own pacifist politics, it returns to its generic roots and ends in a shoot-out wor-thy of any Hollywood production, one that also conveniently removes the barrier to peace from the picture.

A brief comparison with Thaddeus O'Sullivan's *Nothing Personal* illustrates the pitfalls of working within a populist medium that requires both comprehensibility and closure from its narratives. Like *The Boxer*, *Nothing Personal* is set in Belfast just as a ceasefire (this time in 1975) is announced. This evokes a scornful response from the loyalist terrorists at the film's centre, who have been combining a lucrative protection racket with their more ideologically inspired paramilitary activities. A "love-across-the-divide" structure polarises and then suggests a *rapprochement* between two symbolic groupings. On the one hand are the old childhood friends, loyalist Kenny (James Frain) and republican Liam (John Lynch), now separated by the "peace lines" or barricades. On the other, a tentative romance emerges between Kenny's estranged wife, Ann (Maria Doyle Kennedy) and Liam. Through a night of violence, the two sides are offered the opportunity to come together but, as a succession of *denouements* notches up a death toll that ultimately includes Liam's daughter as well as the loyalists, the film's faith in any possible symbolic union of hearts falters. Where the optimistic viewer might like to believe that Liam and Ann will eventually pursue their love affair, the dynamics of the film suggest otherwise. Like *The Boxer*, O'Sullivan's film is loosely generic (this time drawing on the conventions of the gangster film); its visual depiction of Belfast is also remarkably similar. Both films strive to effect a symbolic union of the various local players in the Troubles; both, to varying degrees, fail. The political confusions that mark *The Boxer* and many other films born of the peace process must therefore be read against a background of popular uncertainty as to the real potential for institutional and communal accord within Northern Ireland. These sentiments feed into and disrupt Sheridan's idealistic vision, resulting in a work that is beset by contradictory impulses to the point of failing to achieve any convincing sense of closure.

Chapter Five

Into the West (1992): The Mythic Family

This concluding chapter returns us to the beginning: to Sheridan's first film script, *Into the West,* which was subsequently turned into a successful feature film. Sheridan has said that he could not have directed it at the time as he had not fully worked the story through in his head; the death of his mother also seems to have freed him from his highly sentimental attachment to mother figures and he has suggested that he would now make it into a somewhat different film (see interview). In any case, by the time he had acquired the international status to direct his own script, he had moved on to a much darker vision of the myth of the west of Ireland (*The Field*).

Into the West was initially to have been directed by Robert Dornhelm, but in the end was shot by the English director, Mike Newell. Newell had previously made the period drama, *Dance with a Stranger* (UK, 1984) and *Enchanted April* (1991) and was to become more widely known when he directed *Four Weddings and a Funeral* (1994). It is difficult to see where *Into the West* fits into this very English director's work. Like most practitioners engaged in British cin-

ema, Newell's films return over and over again to the intersection of sexuality and class, whether in a period or a contemporary setting. He was engaged to direct *Into the West* at
a late point in the film's pre-production and it is reasonable
to see him, under these circumstances, as a director-for-
hire. This is not to belittle his contribution to the film and
indeed, freed of Sheridan's own somewhat pedestrian approach to camerawork and editing, *Into the West* is opened
up to a much wider range of visual possibilities. There are,
however, so many pointers within the film to future directions in Sheridan's career as a director, that we may consider *Into the West* as a critical part of his *oeuvre*.

By now it ought to be clear that at the heart of Jim
Sheridan's cinema lies an overriding concern with the institution of the family. It functions on a symbolic level as a
marker of the nation and on a functional level as a point of
audience identification. In the earlier films, these two discourses merged to produce the idealised figure of Christy's
mother in *My Left Foot* and the monstrous patriarch of *The
Field*. The collaborations with Terry George are notable for
their inner tensions, in particular their attempts to integrate
a political message into a family drama format. As Terry
George describes it, "Jim always gets back to basic family
relationships, these primal issues. I go for the political story
and the structure of it" (Webster, 1998: 89). If the early
films are not overtly political in theme, their foregrounding
of family narratives invites a parallel reading of the family as
nation. The broken family emerges as the broken nation,
divided by violence, recoupable, in this instance, through a
fantasy of the all-caring mother.

In *Into the West,* Sheridan laid the foundations for much
of his later work, although this film, with its address to a
younger audience, is arguably more "innocent" than the subsequent scripts (*Into the West* was written before *My Left
Foot* but produced later). He was no stranger to child-

centred fictions, having worked on a children's TV programme, *Motley*, before gong to University College Dublin. Later, in the 1970s, he and Neil Jordan founded the "Children's T. Company" which toured schools and summer festivals. *Into the West* reflects this experience whilst diverting its children's narrative into a fantasy of reuniting the archetypal broken family of the director's life and fictions. This can only be achieved by taking its young protagonists on a journey that is both literal and imagined.

The story is concerned with two children, Ossie (Ciarán Fitzgerald) and Tito Riley (Ruaidhri Conroy) who come from a family of Travellers that has settled in Dublin's high-rise Ballymun flats following the death of the boys' mother. Their father, Papa Riley (Gabriel Byrne), has sunk into a pattern of drinking and neglect and the boys run wild, riding ponies and begging for money on the streets. Counterpointed with their negligent, degraded father is the boys' grandfather, Grandpa Ward (David Kelly) who has maintained the traditional (and somewhat romanticised) ways of the Travellers, living in a horse-drawn caravan and telling stories around the fire. When he draws in to the wasteground where the Ballymun children play, Grandpa Ward brings with him a white horse, Tír na nÓg, to whom Ossie is magically attracted. The children and Tír na nÓg become embroiled in a show-jumping scam and have to flee Dublin. As the boys travel "into the west", they are separately pursued by a corrupt guard (Brendan Gleeson) who is in league with big business interests, and their father, grandfather, and a tracker, Kathleen (Ellen Barkin), from the travelling community.

Before long it becomes clear that the horse, who seems to embody the spirit of their dead mother, is leading the boys. At one point, when they decide to turn back, the horse forces them forward, bringing them to the grave of their mother. When they finally reach the sea, their pursuers descend on them, armed with the accoutrements of modern technology, cars, helicopters and walkie-talkies, against which Papa Riley and the other Travellers are useless. The horse draws Ossie into the sea and it seems that he must drown. An underwater camera shot, however, reveals a female hand stretched out to him, guiding the child to the surface. As Tír na nÓg disappears, Ossie is returned to shore and recovers. The guards leave, fearful of the consequences of having caused a near death, and Papa Riley swears that the children will never be made go back to the Ballymun flats again.

Into the West offers itself to the viewer simultaneously as a social commentary and a supernatural fantasy. The conditions under which the Riley children live, with their drunken, incapable father, are apparently the consequence of losing their mother and of settling in the city. Papa Riley has rejected the primitive way of life of the Travellers, which he appears to blame for the death of his wife. Nothing in the film makes it clear why this should be and we have to make the somewhat contradictory assumption that she would not have died in childbirth if she had had access to the facilities of a modern hospital. It is soon established that Papa Riley's decision was a mistake and that he and the children must return to Traveller life if they are to function as a family. They must also abandon the city in favour of the rural.

This rejection of the modern city, coupled with an anxiety over the institution of the family unit, echoes through recent Irish cinema. In, for instance, the film *Joyriders* (Aisling Walsh, UK, 1988), the central character, Mary (Patricia Kerrigan), is the victim of an abusive marriage. When she reaches the point where she realises that she can no longer cope with the pressures of poverty and familial violence, she gives up her children and leaves Dublin. In the west of Ireland, she can consummate the relationship she has formed with the young joyrider she encountered in Dublin. They move into a dilapidated cottage with an elderly man and acquire traditional rural skills. Once established, they retrieve her children from the city and settle down as a new and happier family unit. This, and many other films, including *Into the West*, reflect a concern that Ireland, with its swift accession to modernity, has lost more than it gained. A similar theme is also evident in contemporary literature, such as Dermot Bolger's *The Journey Home*.

Such a dystopian view of late-twentieth-century life is not unique to Irish society, nor is Sheridan's reverence for the nurturing mother and the unified family. Distrust of modernity and an over-valuation of the nuclear family are embedded in contemporary western culture. In Ireland, as we saw in Chapter One, much of the concern about abandoning the traditions of a rural society was expressed at the level of personal morality. The availability of contraception, and access to abortion and divorce became national issues, particularly in the 1980s, when the script for *Into the West* was written.

At the heart of this discourse lay a question about the role and influence of Catholic beliefs in contemporary Ireland. As these were seen to be eroded, and increasingly discredited, an outbreak of events occurred that seemed to hark back to a more primitive and superstitious relationship with religious practices, notably the "moving statues" phenomenon of the summer of 1985. These apparitions — statues of the Virgin Mary that appeared to move miraculously — were sighted throughout the Republic and drew wide public and media attention. Margaret MacCurtain has suggested that they "were sessions of mass therapy for a society deeply troubled by the fragmentation of cherished and private values" (MacCurtain, 1993: 203). Certainly, many commentators felt that these unexplained visions represented the last gasp of pagan irrationality in the face of the simultaneous upsurge in materialism, on the one hand, and privation on the other. This anxieties emerge in *Into the*

West as a search for a validating metanarrative. As we shall
see below, the lost children of the nation/family are offered
a choice of structuring myths; specifically, those of the he-
roic legends of the Irish past as guaranteed by the spirit/
mother, and the cinematic western.

In Sheridan and Newell's film, the extended Traveller
grouping is elevated to the symbol of the divided family. The
Travellers are caught in a midway place between the traditions with which they have been identified — magical practices, artisanal skills — and the comforts that life within capitalist society offers. Their lifestyle is an anachronism, both in
terms of their representation within the film and outside of
it, since by the early 1990s few Travellers lived in horse-
drawn caravans. Within this fictionalised configuration, the
mother figure assumes primary importance. Without his
wife, Mary, Papa Riley has turned into a drunk; as the children pass through the countryside on the way to the sea,
they pass a statue of the Virgin Mary, to which someone has
attached the motto, "God Bless the Travellers"; and it is the
female tracker, Kathleen, who leads Papa Riley back to his
children. The west of Ireland is specifically associated with
this maternal motif. The white horse appears out of the
ocean as if it was its home and it is in the ocean that Ossie is
reborn through the intervention of his spirit/mother.

This trope was to recur throughout Sheridan's films, as
we have already seen. Nearly all the significant female characters in his scripts are mothers; even Maggie in _The Boxer_ is
identified more as mother than lover. Gareth Peirce is an
exception in that she appears not to be a mother, but is still
awarded sympathetic treatment. Part of the reason that Eileen Cole in _My Left Foot_ is sidelined in terms of soliciting
audience identification is her lack of maternal signifiers,
whilst the Tinker Girl's redeeming features in _The Field_ are
her nurturing tendencies. The difference between the depiction of the Travellers in _The Field_ and _Into the West_ is one of

symbolism. In the former, they represent a malevolent pre-Christianity opposed to the hegemonic practices of society; in the latter, they are more akin to New Age hippies. The spirit/mother persona is drawn indiscriminately from the signifiers of Catholicism and legend. Indeed, this was to be the case throughout Sheridan's work, with institutionalised religious practices either critiqued (Christy's encounter with the priest in *My Left Foot*) or shown to be ineffectual (in *The Field* and *Some Mother's Son*). The structuring legacy of Catholicism remains associated with the Irish psyche, but more as a free-floating signifier. This legacy coexists with an equally potent adherence to ancient superstitious practices; again, to return briefly to *My Left Foot*, we see this when Christy is wheeled by his mother back home from the church and they pass a Hallowe'en bonfire where costumed children dance wildly around burning effigies in the darkness.

The associations between maternity and the redemptive west in *Into the West* are accentuated by the film's vision of Dublin as the corrupt city. Under Newell's guidance, a sharp set of contrasts is established around the divisions between city and countryside. Dublin is visualised as the embodiment of the deprivations of modernity (the Ballymun Towers, the backdrop for the film's urban setting, have become cinematic shorthand for a city that, up until recently, has been consistently associated with poverty and crime). Further, it is seen to be a masculine space, dominated by the phallic towers and regulated by an array of male functionaries, the man from the Welfare, the guards, and the wheeler-dealers with whom Papa Riley does business. In an establishing sequence, Papa Riley drags the two boys over to a campsite where a Traveller family is assuring the representative from the Department of Social Welfare that they have multiple children and are entitled to substantial welfare payments. Their home is a caravan surrounded by debris, the flats looming in the background. Tito and Ossie dutifully pretend to be members

of the Murphy clan before returning to their own flat, with
its mattresses on the floor and the impression of dirt and
abandonment. In this world, only the television set provides
escape from the everyday, and it is on this that the children
watch their beloved westerns.

The first clash between myth and modernity takes place
in this setting, where it is milked for its comic potential. To
the dismay of their neighbours, the children elect to keep
Tír na nÓg in their small flat. When the family next door
objects, Papa Riley, in a rare reminder of why he was once
King of the Travellers, physically threatens the intruders and
dangles one of the men out of his window. He is less effective when the Guards storm his flat and remove the horse.
In the melee that ensues, Tír na nÓg easily kicks through the
paper-thin wall that separates the neighbours from the
Rileys. This hole subsequently allows Ossie and Tito to
watch *Butch Cassidy and the Sundance Kid* (George Roy Hill,
US, 1969) after Papa Riley has confiscated their own set (he
has learnt that the boys have been mitching off school).

This imbrication of the dual myths, of old Ireland and the
American west, is reprised throughout the film. The repeated references to cinema, both as a narrative and as a
location in which to watch those narratives, suggest a level
of self-reflexivity that recognises the fantastical and allegorical nature of the journey the children are undertaking. A
return to the past, as the film acknowledges, is impossible;
even a return to the maternal must remain a dream, and the
children's mother may never actually reappear in corporeal
form.

Early on, Grandpa Ward tells the Traveller children the
story of Oisín who, in Irish legend, went to live in Tír na
nÓg, the land of eternal youth. The narrator inserts his listeners into the narrative by asserting that Oisín was a Traveller and started to miss life on the road and his caravan. He
is told he may return to Ireland and retain his youth and

beauty if he does not set foot on the land. When his saddle breaks, he falls to the ground and withers away into dust. This tale has the function of establishing the symbolic (if a-historical) place of the Travellers in contemporary Ireland, as keepers of the old stories and their heroes. Ossie (Oisín?) is particularly struck by this retelling of the familiar legend and returns to it at intervals during the film.

However, the two boys are equally motivated by their pleasure in old cowboy films. When they set off on their journey, it is to the accompaniment of "Hi, ho, silver!", and they repeatedly refer to themselves as cowboys. As they complete their mythic odyssey, therefore, the boys are faced with two potential sources of identification. They are Oisín, travelling to Tír na nÓg; and they are cowboys riding into the sunset. As Traveller children, the film suggests, they can access either or both legends. Further, they can invent themselves as heroes or victims, cowboys or "Indians", as on several occasions, they ask whether the Travellers are the Indians of Ireland.

Luke Gibbons, in his exploration of the similarities between the myths of the American west and the Irish west of Synge, has distinguished a crucial difference between the two: "In the former . . . it is the community that needs the individual, the hero; in the latter, the individual needs the community" (Gibbons, 1996: 31). Thus, the archetypal western hero, Shane, must turn his back on the community he has saved and ride into the distance; whilst Christy in *The Playboy of the Western World* is motivated only by his desire for acceptance into the community of the islanders.

Into the West does not distinguish between these two sets of myths and its *denouement* is derived from both. This temporal collapsing of historical references is epitomised by the figure of the tracker woman — played by a Hollywood actress dressed in a style that refers indiscriminately to 1960s' counter-culture, native American costume and children's book illustrations of Celtic princesses. In another visual play on the interchangeability of both traditions, we see the Travellers dancing and singing Irish songs around their campfire in the darkness. The children and the dancers run between the seated figures of other Travellers who have dragged old sofas and armchairs outdoors and rigged up a large television set, which they are watching by the light of the fire. Neither group seems remotely inconvenienced by the other. Going back to Gibbons's distinctions, it seems that the children need neither the wilderness nor the community; they need the myth. Although they know that their goal is to reach the west, neither understands why that should be so. They are merely claiming their places in the fiction of the western and the legends they have heard from Grandpa Ward; as cowboys they must go to the Wild West, and, as the mythical Oisín did, they must find Tír na nÓg.

Before they achieve their objective, the children pass through the midlands. This transitional territory separates the city from the west of Ireland, and further functions as a halting post in their voyage. In this liminal space between modernity and tradition, the boys negotiate their way between the two discourses their society has offered them; further, they have to question their own identity as Travellers (cowboys or Indians). This moment of truth is foregrounded by the sequence in which the two boys end up spending the night in the cinema. Tired of playing cowboys and sleeping under the stars, they decide to stay in a hotel. The hotelkeeper, who recognises them as Travellers, refuses them entry. It is now pouring rain and Tito sends Ossie ahead of him into the cinema whilst he waits outside with the horse until the show is over and Ossie can let him in. The movie playing is *Back to the Future III* (Robert Zemeckis, US, 1989), a playful, postmodern take on the theme of the time traveller. In it, teenager Marty McFly (Michael J. Fox) travels back in time to rescue his friend, mad scientist, Dr.

Brown (Christopher Lloyd), who has decided to stay in the past. In the first two parts of the trilogy, McFly has successfully used time travel to reunite his parents and prevent his own (future) children going to jail. In the scenes that Ossie watches and later plays back for Tito, McFly and Brown find themselves pursued through the Wild West in their de Lorean by a rampaging cavalry. Reinvigorated, even possibly reborn, through their night in the cinema, where they learn to control the technology that provides them with their myths — switching on and off the lights, raiding the popcorn machine, running the film — the children too are now prepared to travel back into the past, put the family back together again, defy the law and face the cavalry.

In *Into the West,* Sheridan invites the viewer into a circuit of postmodern knowingness that was not to be repeated in the later films. The film, like *Back to the Future III*, deliberately plays with time and place, drawing as it does on an array of myths and indiscriminately redeploying iconic images of Ireland. However, its potential subversiveness is greatly lessened by its own validation of the myth-making process. Cinema becomes not so much a signifier of the alienating mechanics of capitalist enterprise but rather modernity's own best antidote, the medium which offers escape from the conditions that have produced it.

Like so many of the later films, *Into the West* teeters on the brink between sentimentality and irony. It is most challenged when it relocates its action to the west of Ireland. These scenes can easily be read at face value, as validating the myth of the Celtic fringe. In Sheridan's film, the west of Ireland is the "real" Ireland, the locus of authenticity; it is, however, also a fantasy. *Into the West* opens there and it is to there that it leads its protagonists. In the opening credit sequence, a white horse gallops through the surf under moonlight. As it begins its movement, the soundtrack leads in to the sound of a female voice singing a ballad. Daylight

finds Grandpa Ward sitting on a cluster of rocks at the water's edge from where he greets the horse, who follows him
to Dublin. Named Tír na nÓg after the mythical land of
eternal youth located under the ocean bed, the horse is a
benign dream apparition that has been unconsciously sum-
moned, it seems, by the children and Papa Riley.

In establishing these contrasts between the modern city
and the primitive seascape, *Into the West* appears to situate
itself quite deliberately within an established, even clichéd
representational tradition. The western seaboard has been
annexed by a succession of cultural and political movements
in search of a symbolic representation of pure Irishness.
Thus Yeats, and the writers and artists of the Revival, found
in this remote space a geography of place and mind uncon-
taminated by the modernising processes of the metropolitan
British coloniser or the new Catholic bourgeoisie. Their
successors within the cultural nationalist movement of the
mid-twentieth century were equally determined to find in
the west of Ireland an Irish identity and way of life that
would suit the new, idealised, national self-image. Since then,
the west of Ireland has been appropriated by the Irish Tourist Board as a primitive haven for the largely metropolitan
European and North American visitor. Other groups that
have been drawn to the west in recent years include hippies
and eco-tourists, as well as those who wish to "downsize"
and escape the rat race of the city and the large corporation.
Not only are "virtual" and "real" tourists encouraged by this
discourse to visit a different place; they are also promised a
journey to a different temporal location. Although positioned as a voyage back in time, it is in fact no such thing,
since few participants in the fantasy actually wish to relive
the impoverished life of a nineteenth-century peasant. Instead, it is advertised as an escape from the swift pace of the
late twentieth, early twenty-first centuries into a world
where time is slowed down, where a selection of signifiers

of "pastness" create a temporality that is in fact parallel to that of existing time, not anterior to it.

Cinema, with its appeal to the oneiric, has been central to the establishment of the west as a dream space and time. As has already been discussed in Chapter Two, *The Quiet Man* has played a formative role in giving concrete embodiment to the immigrant, metropolitan fantasy of a return to nature, indeed a union with nature, as symbolised by the romance between Sean Thornton and Kate Danaher. The physical background to the film, the sweeping vistas of lake and mountain, river and sea, are all part of its romantic vision and thus easily redeployed within a tourist discourse that attempts to elide the distinction between image and reality.

A repeated theme in Irish cinema, as we have seen, has been that of escape to the rural, most commonly the west of Ireland. Moreover, cinematic time takes place outside of real time, and the experience of the cinema viewer is analogous to that of the tourist. Both are immersed in a parallel space in which lifetimes can pass by in the course of an hour or two, and the past can be replicated in a sanitised world of unanchored signifiers. Within that space, conflicts are resolved and the incomplete is made whole. More specifically, where the city is commonly associated with marital breakdown, the failure of love and the unhappy childhood, the rural west becomes the panacea for the ills of contemporary culture. The city is also associated with the imposition of an unnatural form of law and order. The guards are portrayed as corrupt and self-serving, arbiters of a justice system that favours the rich over the poor. They constitute a physically threatening presence, intimidating Papa Riley and the children, and forcing the former, under conditions that pre-empt similar scenes in *In the Name of the Father*, to sign a document that will rescind the children's claim to the horse. After they have broken into the Rileys' flat, they forcibly re-

move Tír na nÓg and even his supernatural powers are useless against their weaponry. However, as the action moves
to the west, the representatives of state law become less
powerful as the natural order reasserts itself. This confirms
Luke Gibbons' theory that the west, both in the Irish and
the cinematic sense, exists outside conventional law and order (Gibbons, 1996: 24).

This elevation of the west of Ireland over the metropolitan city as signifier of the authentic and the oneiric is crucial
to *Into the West*. Where, in its middle segment, it suggested
that the children's odyssey was as fictional as that of the
time travellers in *Back to the Future III*, ultimately it embraces
its own fantasy. It was only later, in *The Field*, that Sheridan
revised his vision of the west, rendering it instead as a place
where lawlessness becomes a threat, as opposed to a liber-
ating force, where the maternal is silenced, and where an
overbearing, regressive patriarchal culture runs rampant.
The myth of the male hero, so crucial to *Into the West,* becomes exposed as anachronistic and disabling.

It may not be fanciful to suggest that *Into the West*'s validation of the myth-making function of cinema reflects a personal set of concerns. At the time he was writing it, Sheridan
himself was setting off on his own odyssey, one that would
leave behind the more traditional forms of Irish cultural expression, notably theatre, and embrace the new world of
filmmaking. Like Ossie and Tito, he had abandoned Dublin
and become a traveller, albeit of a different kind. As his father tried to put the family back together through amateur
drama, so Sheridan was to try to do the same via the medium of film. Before he could do so, like the children, he had
to learn to control the medium, to switch the lights on and
off and run the camera. Then he was free to set off on the
fantastical journey that would enable him, in his own way, to
reconstruct the family.

As we have now seen, this journey took him further than he could have imagined, to Hollywood, fame, success and controversy. His filmic validation of the outsider, the individual who must disassociate themselves from the conditions of their upbringing so that they may arrive at a better understanding of their own identity, suggests that he embraces his travelling lifestyle as much as he always returns to Ireland in his fictions.

This book has followed the journey so far but, as it is being written, its subject is shooting his latest film, *East of Harlem*, starring Samantha Morton and Paddy Considine, the love story he has long been planning. The final chapter is clearly far off in the future.

Interview with Jim Sheridan

Ruth Barton: How did you become involved in filmmaking and when did you set up Hell's Kitchen, your production company? I'm not sure how involved you are in production as opposed to directing. Do you put your name to a film and stand back from it? Also, do you still collaborate with Noel Pearson?

Jim Sheridan: I was broke in the Project [Theatre in Dublin, of which he was a founder] in more ways than one and once I got the Project back together again, I decided to go to America because I didn't think that I would really be able to do anything in England other than have a headache. I found that, as much as Ireland is caught up with the same old things, so England is caught up with the other side of the coin and I just wanted to go somewhere where it was much more free. There was nobody you could look to who had gone to America and survived artistically. I don't know anybody who did, maybe John Ford, but you always feel he came back and he was second or third generation. I just liked the idea of going to America, the big pond where I could be the little fish. There was a certain anonymity about going there after running the Project a long time. They were the personal reasons.

I got involved in cinema because I was trying to run the Irish Arts Center in New York and I had always wanted to make films and I was getting nowhere. When I was about 37 or 38 I was really broke and I started writing screenplays to try and get out of the theatre world, which New York exposes for what it is much more than Dublin does. I don't think my concerns are really capable of working through the theatre or I just didn't have the ability to do it. I liked working in small spaces like the Project or the Irish Arts Center, which need government funding to survive and in America you don't have any, so you are more exposed. I went into film and started writing scripts and wrote a script called *Into the West*. Then I wrote *My Left Foot* and when I met the people who were supposed to direct it, I decided I would cast it and direct it myself. Noel Pearson was producing it and it was his idea to start working on something about Christy Brown. There are many myths about that time. The actual truth was that we went over to convince Daniel [Day-Lewis] to play the part — I had sent the script to him via the girl in Noel's office and she sent it without the covering note and that fascinated Daniel. He got on to Noel and Noel said I wanted to direct it and he wasn't against it, so we went over and met him. Then he said he wouldn't do it and he would do it and we had to convince him to do it. We went to a meeting in his agent's office to sign Daniel's contract and he opened the champagne and at that point I said to Noel, "Look, if Daniel signs the contract before I sign mine to direct, then I'm not going to do it." We had a big row there, outside the office and Julian, his agent, looked at us, like, you know . . . and so we went out on the street and had a big argument, me, Noel and Shane Connaughton [the co-scriptwriter]. Noel said, "Well, I suppose you can direct it." And we went back in and Daniel signed and that's how I got to direct it.

RB: Had you had your eye on Daniel from his filmmaking or his theatre career?

JS: I never saw him in the theatre.

RB: So, it was from films like *My Beautiful Laundrette*?

JS: It was his entrance in *My Beautiful Laundrette*. You can tell within thirty seconds on the screen whether somebody is good, whether they have star quality and he was a star even then; but he wasn't known in America.

RB: How did Hell's Kitchen start?

JS: I started that in about '92 to make *In the Name of the Father*, which I was doing on my own. I'd had a row with Noel.

RB: So that's when you stopped working with Noel?

JS: Yes; and to answer your question, would I work again with Noel? I would if there was a project. He's very charismatic and very good at getting the money and very talented. A lot of his heart is really in the theatre and not in the film world. The thing about Noel is that he has a huge artistic ability but not for things like scriptwriting. It's not that he wouldn't have a good idea about how a story should be told but he'd never write it and I think that he sometimes thinks that it's a lot easier than it is. I read a few things he has recently and he has a really good story about Philip Lynott [of the band Thin Lizzy] and a good story about Sam Beckett. The funny thing is that he is trying to discover these writers who will be good writers for screenplays. I would have no trouble working with him. The fight we had about eight years ago wasn't so much a fight as a disagreement, just a totally different way of seeing things. (In a way, I grew up, business-wise, that time. I didn't care about the business side of it but I learned that I had to, because a lot of film is about that. You have to know the ins and outs of it.)

RB: You set up your own production company so that you would have more control over what you do?

JS: Yes, so that I would have a company to make it under.

RB: At what point did you decide to take on films that you would not direct and what pushed you to produce your own?

JS: I suppose in a way I thought I could get some Irish films going and help some people to make films and help my brother [Peter Sheridan]. The problem gets to be that you spend as much time producing a film if you get involved as you do when you are directing and writing. Then there's the avoidance. It was particularly hard for me because of the relationship I had with Daniel and, to an extent, Noel. They were very creative and very tense. It was hard work making a film and I think unconsciously, you avoid it. I do. So, in a way, I wasted a bit of time doing all that producing. Something like *The Mammy* [aka *Agnes Browne,* directed by and starring Anjelica Huston in 1999] is great and you didn't say, "What am I doing here?" But I do think, from all that experience, it isn't possible to start an Irish film industry or production company that will be successful right now. I think the basic reason for that is the lack of co-ordination between RTÉ and the filmmakers. (I think all the Irish films should be made for TV and just screened that way initially and if they are successful then distributed internationally. There's nothing to stop people doing that. Instead they do it the other way round. They make films, float them about internationally and then they are not capable of being shown on RTÉ. So the people who are putting up the money, the taxpayers, have no way of judging what they are actually putting up the money for. You get the classic dilemma. It's for the children of the rich. I don't mean the children of the rich in any disparaging sense, in that class-based way at all. I just mean that it's a fact that well educated people can make a lot of grant applications. It shouldn't cost as much, making a film. Our market can't support that level of filmmaking. You can have a successful film from $50,000 to $50 million. I wish there was some company that could get things together where there would be income to make films.

RB: But RTÉ say they can't support filmmaking and that it doesn't make them any money. They can only make money out of mini-series. So, as far as they are concerned, it's not their problem.

JS: Nothing is RTÉ's problem. They have never produced a successful anything in thirty years, anything, not even a quiz show. They haven't produced anything that has gone international. It's the most unproductive . . . well I don't want to get into that. There are a lot of people in RTÉ that are very good. It's the organisation.

RB: I read an interview where you said that you wanted to break with the Irish literary tradition and make the classic three-act structured film. And that was also the time when the predominant filmmaking culture, such as it was, was an avant-garde one, with people like Pat Murphy and Bob Quinn making that type of film. So you were also breaking with that tradition. Why did you decide to go outside the parameters of Irish literature and Irish film?

JS: I suppose the Irish literary tradition has influenced me more than anything else. When I do films I go back to Irish literature a lot. I always go back to James Joyce, and to an extent Synge. I never go back to Sean O'Casey, which is weird. For me there's not much in that. That is probably the world I was caught up in Dublin, whereas the mythological world of Synge and Yeats and Joyce is much closer to cinema. James Joyce always tells me the answer to everything I need to know on any project I'm doing. He wanted to be a dramatist himself but he didn't because of Ibsen and I always wonder why he didn't. There was a bit of competition with Ibsen but it went deeper than that. If you read his appraisal of Shakespeare in *Ulysses*, you just know this guy knew everything about writers even before it was researched. He had that instinct.

I realised that making a film set in Ireland or England and trying to make it work in America or the rest of the world, you had to have a theme or a sub-structure that would appeal on a deeper level. So, I'd always find myself thinking of a story. In *My Left Foot* I was always thinking of the oedipal bit and in *In the Name of the Father* I was thinking of the Good Father. In this one now, I'm thinking of a love story. I had to think when was the oedipal story ever told, when was the Good Father ever told in Ireland? When was a love story ever told? And if I could find that they really weren't ever told, then I'd be happy. The answer to the Good Father is that Leopold Bloom was probably the best father in Irish history, in terms of internal politics and morality and I think Joyce was smart to make him Jewish. Up to Roddy Doyle, I suppose there was really no Good Father, which is why the name Guiseppe in the Conlon story appealed. It's a kind of weird name, somehow outside of the Irish thing.

RB: In *The Field* you have a very bad father.

JS: Yes, and that didn't work internationally. That plays into the Cuchulainn myth and, although those myths are really branches of the main European story system, they haven't really managed to make their way into the tree, into mainstream literature. I think they are too unique to Ireland. I am actually writing another story about a father, but I'm trying to make a film about a Hitler figure, which worries me. It is very like *The Field*. But I didn't see him [the Bull McCabe] as a bad father necessarily, just as misguided. It was a powerful story and many people like it the best of all the films. I think that might be an Irish thing — they get it. I'm not sure it works outside. I'm now trying to do a love story. It's difficult to find an Irish love story. Now Joyce always made love stories about women in love with dead people which I think has something to do with the national psychic mood, where the only true love is dead. That's true from Nora to the women of *The Dead* to Molly Bloom. I started writing this story about my own time in America and I made myself my father and my wife my mother which may say something about me that I don't want printed. And then because my brother died when I was a kid, then I brought that into the story. I realised that the story was about the husband and the wife and a triangle with their dead child and this couple has gone to America to get rid of this death culture. It sounds easy to write a love story and it sounds like it should be possible. But it doesn't seem to be easy in Ireland. There seem to be strong women and drunken fathers. Joyce said an Irishman's home is his coffin, as opposed to his castle.

Avant-garde filmmaking? The trouble with that is that even if you look at avant-garde writing, it happened straight after the war and then receded. The war experience was far more profound than anything since then. That's over now. It's hard to trust art when it's funded by a government source, because it's like poetry. You can do it for nothing. *The Blair Witch Project* was made for $30,000. You just make things that make it easier for people to get up and go home after the cinema. You just make it to make life easier. In ways I admire all those Hollywood moguls. I can't believe they did it just for commercial reasons. I know Harvey Weinstein [co-founder of Miramax] and he is the toughest monster of them all and he has a greater love of cinema than anyone I have met in the avant-garde. I can never believe that came of wanting to rip off the public.

RB: Your first films were made for British television. Then you started being funded by Hollywood. Do you think that that has changed the kind of films you make and the way you make them?

JS: Well, you couldn't have made *In the Name of the Father* for British television. I was very happy with that one in that regard and the more the British press went mad at me, the happier I was. The thing about that was that everyone lived with the fact that the IRA couldn't be on television. So they were used to not being allowed to say anything and suddenly they see this film and it's like from outer space. It's kind of saying what they want to say and they are afraid to say, although they wouldn't exactly say it the way I did it. The IRA man would have been nicer in the film! But I think it was a shock as much to them as it was to the British system. That also made me happy. The fundamental of that film was that a pacifist father took control. That's what makes it good. Far from being a thing that they [the British] should have been against, they should have embraced it. I was asked why I had changed the facts and no matter how many times I explained it, they always came back to the same thing — why did I put the father and son in the same cell? Now, apart from the fact that they actually were in the same cell for a short amount of time and in the same prison for months, the question itself fascinated me because after a while I would say to them, "Well, maybe you are right but I have actually shown you in a more humane position than you actually were in and you seem angry that I did that. So why are you angry that I made you seem more humane than you actually were? Is it that you don't consider yourselves the same species of human being that are in the cells?" And they don't see and we don't see what the racism is about. It's strange and it's still there and it's pathetic and we should oppose it and not be afraid to oppose it. I actually think that the verbal opposition disarms the violence and therefore the more you talk about it in pictures, the more control you have over the uncontrollable.

RB: Is it a problem making Troubles films? I was reading reviews of *The Boxer*, for instance, that mostly started off saying that, despite this being a film about the Troubles, it was still very good; indeed, the British reviews were very positive. There seemed to be an assumption of audience resistance to films about the Troubles.

JS: *The Boxer* I did as a reaction to *In the Name of the Father* in many ways. Daniel wanted to make a boxing film and if I wasn't going to make a commercial American film, then I was going to make a film that had another look at the North in the context of where it was at and I wanted to endorse the people who were giving up violence. That's what it is about. It's a propaganda film made with Hollywood money and, OK, it lost money but it did some social good, I think, I hope. You never know. Everyone thinks that the Americans don't understand why the Protestants and Catholics fight. They do, they totally do. They just don't want to pay attention. They think, "Hold on, we left England four hundred years ago to get away from this shit. Why are we going back? Why are we paying money to go back on *The Mayflower*?" They don't want to go back. It's a resistance of spirit, not of intellect. The Europeans always think, "the stupid Americans". It's not that. The Americans can work it out if they need to; it's just that spiritually they are not interested. So it has a very limited audience.

RB: Are you always thinking about an American audience? Is a British audience not money-making enough?

JS: I'm not interested really in that [British] audience. They seem to dwell in another century. I want to be where the breaking wave is. (I think American cinema has destroyed other cultures) Some of those cultures deserve to be destroyed and are just the wrecks of history but a lot of good grows out of that. In the sense of how people live, they live through television now; that's their ethics and morals, not the Pope or anything. I always tell this story about how my father put up the television aerial . . .

RB: I read about it in your brother's book.

JS: And the conclusion was that the signal from England for the BBC was being blocked by the church. If you take away the church, and the school that was next door, you're left with the television. What we see on the television dictates the way we live. Our morals and ethics are dictated by Hollywood and MTV.

RB: So, why do you do Troubles films?

JS: If you ask me what's wrong with Troubles films it is that they don't go far enough. The Irish audience want *Michael Collins* but they want Michael Collins to live. All tribes with a savage instinct want the killer to eradicate the others quickly to get it over with but given that that can't be done and that that may not necessarily be right, it then becomes very difficult to make those films because you are now making a gangster film or another genre film. I think there still are fascinating films to be made about the North but how they would fit in to have more resonance, I don't know. They will be made eventually when we have a bit of distance from it.

RB: One of the things that comes through all your films, and it starts with *My Left Foot*, is the story of a young man who attempts to break free of his background. Is that drawn from your own experience?

JS: Probably. Even though we lived in a poor area, we were the aristocrats of that area, the well-off family, due a lot to my mother running a lodging house, my da working two jobs. I often feel that we had an extended family, with the lodgers and all. I'm not sure the nuclear family is a healthy thing. It's a classic story: somebody comes out against the odds. I think it's more like a spiritual thing again. I love Christy Brown. In some way, you are allowed tell the Christy Brown story because he's so crippled. The audience will allow you tell that story out of their culture because of his unique physical condition that somehow mirrors an interior emotional condition. Although it's about a real person, it works because he has a great spirit even though he's disenfranchised physically. It's like he is the reverse of that oedipal character; that means swollen foot, and it's like the curse the father put on the son; in this case, the wound is so big that the only thing left is the foot. I think that, in this culture, he would be fed and nourished by this particular group of people; that says a lot about how the people who nourish him see themselves as well, more out of love than fear; empathy is fear converted I feel.

RB: You gave him a far more caring background than comes through in the books, particularly in *Down All the Days*, which is a nightmarish story.

JS: The real Christy Brown had the clearest eyes you have ever seen. I always felt — this is the part of the interview where people say, "he's really cracked" — that he was caring for me even after he was dead, in weird ways. But those eyes were the most piercing eyes I ever saw in all of Ireland. I read *Down All the Days* and I'm going, "What is going on here?" We did it as a play, me and my brother, four or five years before, and it was hugely unsuccessful. It took place when the hunger strikes were on. It lost money and nobody went to see it. It started with a funeral. The father is a monster. He beats up the mother when she is pregnant, but Christy never brings this further and asks the question, was my condition incurred because of this kind of beating? In reality, when Christy saw a documentary about himself, he was shocked and horrified when he saw that he looked like he did because, even though he shook, his eyes were still. So, you can imagine, the clearest eyes at the still centre of the earth, even though his body was shaking. He saw himself as perfect. And he never went to that place where he fully addressed his embryonic background, so I know that the book has a Tom Wolfe avalanche of words. It's very well written, maybe a little bit over-written and not getting to the kernel. In a way, we were lucky we only had *My Left Foot* rights-wise — it forced me not to go back to *Down All the Days.*

It's funny, when you are distilling something from a story into a film. Stories are like the structures of houses. They have a top floor where all the talk goes on, an attic where the interior monologue goes on. Films have no attic. It's like *The Deer Hunter* [Michael Cimino, 1978]; it's a structure on bamboo sticks that is capable of collapsing any minute. If you take one out, it will fall. The structure at the top is not like a monument, or a great work of literature. It's balanced on the most precarious foundations. It's very hard to get a story that works.

I would say *The Quiet Man* surpasses every other Irish work of art in important aspects in that it's a true, genuine love story and in the beginning of the love story, the guy has killed somebody in a fair fight and he comes back to protect the woman from the incest culture. *The Playboy of the Western World* is the story where he's supposed to kill his father, all the women fall in love with him, they find he didn't kill him so they hate him, he kills him again, he hates them. It turns out he's still not dead and they go out together. It's always a tragic story played out as farce and not attaining love story status because you can't get past the first stage of initiation. John Ford just got it, bang! And that had to do with the fact that he was a liberated American and what we hate in that film, those characters, they exist and they existed in Ford's time, and if they didn't exist as Ford saw them, which was a little bit malarkey, they exist as types and it's a mirror that the Irish don't want to look into.

RB: I always think that, in *The Field*, you were putting that world of *The Quiet Man* onto the screen again. It's set in the same area with the same kind of people; there's the American who comes back to assert his birthright, except that in *The Field* he doesn't get White O'Morn or the Irish girl and he gets killed.

JS: Maybe I should have really bastardised poor old John B.'s play and had the American get the tinker girl. That would have been fabulous. That would have been a hit! The funny thing about that story is that it is about emotions that are very hard to understand, that need for land. Americans can look at themselves leaving that embassy in Phnom Penh [in

Roland Joffé's *The Killing Fields*, GB, 1984] and have no problem with it. The Irish and the British would be hiding their
heads for the next fifty years. How can you look at those
people in the helicopters getting beaten down and still live
with that? Their culture is about moving on from problems,
leaving them behind, forgetting them.

RB: Most of your films are set in the past. Even *The Boxer*
was set in the recent past. Why do you do that?

JS: That's interesting . . . I was just sitting there thinking why
do I do these interviews — not necessarily with you! — and
I was thinking, I don't have an agenda in doing them. I'm actually, in a funny way, talking to myself, trying to figure out
what I actually think and the part of me that does have any
agenda is always the part that I think is going to come out
bad. Everything seems to me to be about emotional vulnerability. That seems to be what the audience wants. They just
want to see into the soul. A lot of the time, we are just
afraid of that. We don't like who we are. Stars are about
self-esteem, writing is about self-esteem. Everything is about
twisted self-esteem. The more I see it . . . what was the
question?

RB: Why do you set your films in the past?

JS: Now, that's interesting. The story I am doing now is
about my own life and really, to be commercial it should be
about now, it should be about America now. Martin
Scorsese made *Bringing Out the Dead* a year or so ago [1999]
and you're going through New York and you're saying,
where is that New York? He says it's the early nineties;
maybe. But that thing of the fearful place, it's more traditional and I'm setting it back a bit to get more of that. But,
the actual truth is that films don't live on in the past, they

are always in the future. Their dialogue with the audience is future-based, referring back. When you say "action", you can't say "action past"; you mean action in the future. You are creating a reality in the future tense that is going to sit there playing this way. It's not necessarily about the past, it's about where we are now. The further it is ahead of the present, the longer it seems to last. So I never feel they are about the past in that sense. The past is only a territory. It's only a backdrop. *The Field* is only about the past in so much as it's probably really about the IRA and nationalism and what it all means, at a real level. For me it's not really about the past.

RB: It's been suggested that you did that to please foreign backers.

JS: No, there was no necessity on me to do that. I felt the emotions that I wanted to get for *The Field* were very hard to get in the 1960s. I didn't want to go into the pub. I didn't want to have all those conversations, those subsidiary characters. I had to find a world that could externalise those interior needs. That was a primitive need manifested in a modern context. It's very hard to do. Ray McAnally wanted the Bull to be much less sympathetic.

RB: I think he is great because he is so sympathetic. You are drawn to him and you understand what he is doing but he is wrong and in the end he destroys everything.

JS: The funny thing is, I wanted him to be less sympathetic than Richard [Harris] wanted him to be. That was an argument between us. And that comes over when the plot point turns in the first act. I think Richard thought that, when he gives out to the priest and the American, you suddenly see his reason for it. And I only wanted to see his mania. I wanted that moment when you know you are in the control of a psychopath. And I don't know if he's right or I'm right, in terms of how many people would go and see it. For me, when stuff is as powerful as voodoo, it's beyond ken, it's beyond comprehension. You get that in great writing, not in many dramatic structures.

RB: Were you happy with the adaptation of *Into the West*?

JS: You mean what Mike Newell did? Yes, I think he did a good job. The reason I didn't do it was I never worked the story out. I have often thought of re-doing it, not because I thought he did it wrong, but I never got to the conclusion of where the story should go. It's kind of based on my mother's life. I unconsciously knew there was something about her birth and as I wrote it I found out that her mother died as she gave birth to my mother. Now that my mother is dead, I think I could rewrite it. It's about a mother spirit as benevolent. But if I was to redo it, I would probably do it slightly differently. The funniest thing is that the mothers in all the films I have done have been amazingly strong, which my mother was, but we were so close, me and her, that there was a slight thing where she loved me too much and that warped me a bit, if that can do it, and I would love to put a bit of that in.

Dublin, Wednesday, 27 June 2001

Jim Sheridan: Filmography

As Director

My Left Foot

Director: Jim Sheridan; Producer: Noel Pearson; Script: Jim Sheridan, Shane Connaughton; Cinematographer: Jack Conroy; Editor: J. Patrick Duffner
Cast: Daniel Day-Lewis, Ray McAnally, Brenda Fricker, Ruth McCabe, Fiona Shaw, Hugh O'Conor
United Kingdom, 1989

The Field

Director: Jim Sheridan; Producer: Noel Pearson; Script: Jim Sheridan; Cinematographer: Jack Conroy; Editor: J. Patrick Duffner
Cast: Richard Harris, John Hurt, Tom Berenger, Sean Bean, Frances Tomelty, Brenda Fricker
United Kingdom, 1990

In the Name of the Father

Director: Jim Sheridan; Producer: Jim Sheridan; Script: Terry
George, Jim Sheridan; Cinematographer: Peter Biziou;
Editor: Gerry Hambling
Cast: Daniel Day-Lewis, Emma Thompson, Pete
Postlethwaite, John Lynch
Ireland/United Kingdom/US, 1993

The Boxer

Director: Jim Sheridan; Producer: Jim Sheridan, Arthur
Lappin; Script: Jim Sheridan, Terry George;
Cinematographer: Chris Menges; Editor: Gerry Hambling,
Clive Barrett
Cast: Daniel Day-Lewis, Emily Watson, Brian Cox, Ken
Stott, Gerard McSorley
Ireland/United Kingdom/US, 1997

East of Harlem

Director: Jim Sheridan; Producer: Jim Sheridan, Arthur
Lappin; Script: Jim Sheridan; Cinematographer: Declan
Quinn; Editor: Naomi Geraghty
Cast: Samantha Morton, Paddy Considine, Djimon Hounsou
To be released

As scriptwriter

Into the West

Director: Mike Newell; Producer: Jonathan Cavendish, Tim
Palmer; Script: Jim Sheridan; Cinematographer: Tom Sigel;
Editor: Peter Boyle
Cast: Gabriel Byrne, Ellen Barkin, Ciarán Fitzgerald, Ruaidhri
Conroy
Ireland, 1992

Some Mother's Son

Director: Terry George; Producer: Jim Sheridan, Arthur Lappin, Edwin Burke; Script: Terry George, Jim Sheridan; Cinematographer: Geoffrey Simpson; Editor: Craig McKay
Cast: Helen Mirren, Fionnuala Flanagan, Aidan Gillen, David O'Hara, John Lynch
Ireland/US, 1996

As Producer

Agnes Browne

Director: Anjelica Huston; Producer: Anjelica Huston, Jim Sheridan, Arthur Lappin, Greg Smith; Script: John Goldsmith, Brendan O'Carroll; Cinematographer: Anthony B. Richmond; Editor: Éva Gárdos
Cast: Anjelica Huston, Marion O'Dwyer, Niall O'Shea, Ciaran Owens
Ireland, 1999

On the Edge

Director: John Carney, Producer, Ed Guiney, Arthur Lappin, Jim Sheridan; Script: John Carney, Daniel James; Cinematographer: Eric Alan Edwards, Editor: Dermot Diskin
Cast: Cillian Murphy, Tricia Vessey, Jonathan Jackson
Ireland, 2000

Bibliography

Allen, K. (2000), *The Celtic Tiger*, Manchester and New York: Manchester University Press.

Andrews, N. (1991), review of *The Field*, *The Financial Times*, 14 February, p. 19.

Backus, M.G. (1999), "Revising Resistance" in J. MacKillop (ed.), *Contemporary Irish Cinema*, Syracuse, New York: Syracuse University Press, pp. 54–70.

Barton, R. (2001), "The Smaller Picture", *Film Ireland*, issue 82, August/September, pp. 30–2.

Bennett, R. (1998), "Don't Mention the War: Culture in Northern Ireland" in D. Miller (ed.), *Rethinking Northern Ireland*, London and New York: Longman, pp. 199–210.

Bew, P. and G. Gillespie (1999), *Northern Ireland, A Chronology of the Troubles, 1968–1999*, revised edition, Dublin: Gill & Macmillan.

Bradshaw, B. (1994), "Nationalism and Historical Scholarship in Modern Ireland" in C. Brady (ed.), pp. 191–216.

Brady, C. (ed.) (1994), *Interpreting Irish History, The Debate on Historical Revisionism, 1938–1994*, Dublin: Irish Academic Press.

Brown, C. (1970), *Down All The Days*, London: Secker and Warburg.

Canby, V. (1990), review of *The Field*, *The New York Times*, 21 December, Section C, p. 14.

Carty, C. (1989), "'I'm Glad You Told Me How To Speak So That I Could Tell You Off'", *The Sunday Tribune*, 26 February, p. 19.

Cleary, J. (1996), "'Fork-Tongued on the Border Pit': Partition and the Politics of Form in Contemporary Narratives of the Northern Irish Conflict", *The South Atlantic Quarterly*, volume 95, number 1, Winter, pp. 227–276.

Conlon, G. (1990), *Proved Innocent*, London: Hamish Hamilton.

Corliss, R. (1998), "What if Rocky Fought All the IRA Bad Guys?", *Time*, 12 January, p. 84.

Cruise O'Brien, C. (1999), reprinted, "Patriot Games" in A. Rosenthal, (ed.), *Why Docudrama?*, Carbondale and Edwardsville: Southern Illinois University Press, pp. 311–15.

Curtis, L. and M. Jempson (1993), *Interference on the Airwaves: Ireland, the Media and the Broadcasting Ban*, London: Campaign for Press and Broadcasting Freedom, pp. 42–92.

Curtis, Q. (1994), "Jim Sheridan's Rage of Innocence", *Independent on Sunday*, 13 March, p. 25.

Dean, J. (1994), "The Far Side — American Letter", *Film West*, issue 18, July, pp. 14–15.

Doyle, D. (1998), "*The Boxer* fails to deliver US knock-out", *The Sunday Tribune*, 8 February, p. 4.

Dwyer, M. (1989), "A Triumphant and Moving *Left Foot*", *The Irish Times*, 24 February, p. 12.

Dwyer, M. (1990), "The Power and the Glory of *The Field*", *The Irish Times*, 21 September, p. 10.

Dwyer, M. (1993), "The Shooting of Gerry Conlon", *The Irish Times*, 8 May, Weekend Section, p. 1.

Feldman, A. (1991), *Formations of Violence*, Chicago and London: The University of Chicago Press.

Fennell, D. (1994), "Against Revisionism" in C. Brady (ed.), pp. 183–190.

Fleischmann, M. (1991), review of *The Field*, *Village Voice*, 1 January, p. 62.

Foster, R. (2001), *The Irish Story*, London: Allen Lane, The Penguin Press.

Georgakas, D. and L. Rubenstein (1983), *The Cineaste Interviews*, Chicago: Lake View Press.

George, T. (1996), *Some Mother's Son* (letter to the editor), *The Irish Times*, 1 October, p. 15.

Gibbons, L. (1996), *Transformations in Irish Culture*, Cork: Cork University Press.

Grenier, R. (1999), reprinted, "In the Name of the IRA", in A. Rosenthal (ed.), *Why Docudrama?*, Carbondale and Edwardsville: Southern Illinois University Press, pp. 316–23.

Harnden, T. (1997), "'Pro-IRA' film costs Helen Mirren role on Lottery Show", *The Daily Telegraph*, 9 January, p. 2.

Harris, E. (1998), "Why truth has been on the ropes", *The Sunday Times*, 1 February, Section 11, pp. 2–3.

Hill, J. (1987), "Images of Violence" in K. Rockett, L. Gibbons, J. Hill, pp. 147–93.

Hill, J. (1999), "Filming in the North", *Cineaste*, volume xxiv, numbers 2–3, pp. 26–7.

Hobsbawm, E. (1995), *Age of Extremes*, second edition, London: Abacus.

Hunter, B. (1998), "Day-Lewis delivers My Left Hook", *The Belfast Telegraph*, 3 February, p. 12.

Innes, C.L. (1993), *Woman and Nation in Irish Literature and Society, 1880–1935,* Athens: University of Georgia Press.

The Irish News (1998), uncredited review of *The Boxer,* 6 February, p. 13.

Johnston, T. (1996), review of *Nothing Personal, Sight and Sound,* volume 6, issue 2, February, pp. 50–1.

Kael, P. (1989), "The Current Cinema, Satyr", *The New Yorker,* volume 65, issue 33, 2 October, pp. 98–100.

Keane, D. (1993), "Sorry, Emma: You're Crazy to do this Film", *Mail on Sunday,* 7 November, p. 33.

Keane, J.B. (1991) *The Field,* revised text, Cork: Mercier Press.

Kenny, M. (1993), "Inside Story of a Sort", *Daily Telegraph,* 18 December, p. 18.

Kiberd, D. (1996), *Inventing Ireland,* first published 1995, London: Vintage.

Klady, L. (1991), "Hollywood counts the cost", *Screen International,* 11–17 January, number 789, p. 11.

Laffan, M. (1991), "Insular Attitudes: The Revisionists and their Critics", in M. Ní Dhonnchadha and T. Dorgan (eds.) *Revising the Rising,* Derry: Field Day, pp. 106–121.

Lee, J.J. (1989), *Ireland 1912–1985,* Cambridge: Cambridge University Press.

Linehan, H. (1993/94), "Getting Out of Jail", *Film Ireland,* issue 38, December/January, pp. 12–14.

Lloyd, D. (1993), *Anomalous States,* Dublin: The Lilliput Press.

Lloyd, D. (1999), *Ireland After History,* Cork: Cork University Press.

MacCurtain, M. (1993), "Moving Statues and Irish Women" in A. Smyth (ed.), *Irish Women's Studies Reader,* Dublin: Attic Press, pp. 203–13.

Malcolm, D. (1991), review of *The Field,, The Guardian*, 21 February, p. 27.

Martin, G. (1997), "Get Martyr", *New Musical Express*, 18 January, p. 25.

Maslin, J. (1993), "The Sins of a Son Are Visited on His Father", *The New York Times*, 29 December, Section C, p. 11, 19.

McAlpine, C. (1993), "Gross injustice forces Sheridan to tell Conlon's chilling story", *The Irish News*, 17 December, p. 11.

McAvera, B. (1988), Catalogue introduction to *Directions Out*, no publisher supplied.

McIlwaine, E. (1993), "Guildford Four film premiere is set for Belfast", *The Belfast Telegraph*, 13 December, p. 1.

McLoone, M. (1994), "*In the Name of the Father*", *Cineaste*, volume xx, number 4, pp. 44–7.

McLoone, M. (2000), *Irish Film, The Emergence of a Contemporary Cinema*, London: British Film Institute.

Medved, M. (1993), "A Case of Holy Terror", *New York Post*, 29 December, p. 32.

Millar, P. (1994), "The Camera that Lies", *The Sunday Times*, 6 February, Section 9, pp. 2 & 4.

Mitchell, G. (1998), "Red, White and very Blue", *The Irish Times*, 27 March, p. 13.

Myler, T. (1991), "'*Field*' year's top-grossing film", *The Hollywood Reporter Weekly International Edition*, 5 February, p. 1–3.

Nash, C. (1997), "Embodied Irishness" in B. Graham (ed.), *In Search of Ireland, A Cultural Geography*, London and New York: Routledge, pp. 108–127.

Nolan, B., P.J. O'Connell and C.T. Whelan (2000), *Bust to Boom?*, Dublin: Institute of Public Administration.

Pearson, N. (1998), "Home and Away", *Film Ireland*, issue 66, August/September, p. 18.

Petley, J. (1981), "Costa-Gavras The Political Thriller", *The Movie*, issue 81, pp. 1616–17.

Rainer, P. (1990), review of *The Field*, *Los Angeles Times*, 20 December, Calendar, p. 11.

Rockett, E. and K. Rockett (2002), *Neil Jordan*, Dublin: The Liffey Press, forthcoming.

Rockett, K., L. Gibbons, and J. Hill (1987), *Cinema and Ireland*, London & Sydney: Croom Helm.

Rockett, K. (1994), "Culture, Industry and Irish Cinema" in J. Hill, M. McLoone, P. Hainsworth (eds.), *Border Crossing, Film in Ireland, Britain and Europe*, Belfast: Institute of Irish Studies/BFI, pp. 126–39.

Romney, J. (1994), "Missed Opportunity", *New Statesman and Society*, 11 February, pp. 35–6.

Schlesinger, P., G. Murdock, and P. Elliott, (1983), *Televising "Terrorism"*, London: Comedia.

Screen International (1991), box office figures for *The Field*, number 800, 29 March, p. 31.

Screen International (1994), box offices figures for *In the Name of the Father*, number 953, 15 April, p. 50.

Sheridan, J. (1989), "Words, Pictures and Buildings", *Film Base News*, issue 12, April/May, pp. 10–12.

Sheridan, P. (1999), *44*, London, Basingstoke and Oxford: Macmillan.

Sheridan, P. (2001), *Forty-seven Roses*, London, Basingstoke and Oxford: Macmillan.

Special Working Group on the Film Production Industry (1992), *The Film Production Industry in Ireland*, Dublin: Government Stationery Office.

Stern, C. and V. Davis (1994), "Hollywood has put us in the dock . . . this torture stuff is pure fantasy", *Mail on Sunday,* 2 January, pp. 48–9.

Sugden, J. and S. Harvie (1995), *Sport and Community Relations in Northern Ireland,* University of Ulster: Centre for the Study of Conflict.

Tansey, P. (1998), *Ireland at Work: Economic Growth and the Labour Market, 1987–1997,* Dublin: Oak Tree Press.

Turan, K. (1993), "The Right Actor for the Wrong Man", *Los Angeles Times,* 29 December, Calendar, p. 1.

Wallace, A. (2001), "Writing Blue Murder", *The Irish Times,* 30 June, Weekend, p. 6.

Webster, A. (1998), "Ireland Unfree . . .", *Premiere,* January, pp. 86–9, 101.

White, A. (1996), "Those *Riverdance* Feet", *The Irish Times,* 25 September, p. 14.

Williams, R. (1998), "My Right Hook", *The Guardian,* 20 February, Section 2, p. 8.

Woodworth, P. (1994), "It's the way he tells 'em . . .", *The Irish Times,* 10 March, Weekend, p. 1.

Young, R. (1993), "Fear Not", *The Belfast News Letter,* 17 December, p. 13.

Zizek, S. (1993), "From Courtly Love to *The Crying Game*", *New Left Review,* number 202, November/December, pp. 95–108.

Suggestions for Further Reading

There are no other books published to date on Jim Sheridan. The main textbooks on Irish cinema currently in print are:

MacKillop, J. (ed.) (1999), *Contemporary Irish Cinema,* Syracuse, New York: Syracuse University Press.

McLoone, M. (2000), *Irish Film, The Emergence of a Contemporary Cinema*, London: British Film Institute.

Pettitt, L. (2000), *Screening Ireland*, Manchester: Manchester University Press.

McIlroy, B. (1998), *Shooting to Kill*, Trowbridge: Wiltshire.

The following publication is out of print but still widely referenced:

Rockett, K., L. Gibbons, J. Hill, (1987), *Cinema and Ireland*, London & Sydney: Croom Helm.

For an exhaustive listing of Irish films and films with an Irish connection, see:

Rockett, K. (1996), *The Irish Filmography*, Dublin: Red Mountain Press.

Index

"west", mythologies of the, 125,
126, 129, 130–3, 134, 135–6
Whelan, Bill, 29, 82
When the Sky Falls, 11
Whitaker, T.K., 17
White, Andy, 82, 101
Who Bombed Birmingham?, 68
Williams, R., 115
Winterbottom, Michael, 120
Wise, Robert, 109
With or Without You, 120
Witness, 102
women, representations of, 23–6,
56–7, 107, 108, 126, 127, 128–9

Woodward, Tim, 81
Woodworth, Paddy, 7
words and language, 96–7
Words upon the Window Pane, 11
"working class boy made good"
theme, 8, 28–9, 149
working-class life, 6–8, 112–14

Yeats, W.B., 42, 144
Young, R., 93

Z, 72
Zemeckis, Robert, 132
Zizek, S., 3